Learning about

LIFE

Learning about LIFE

LOVE, INFATUATION, FRIENDSHIP, EXPLOITATION

A Family-Based Program
on Relationships and Abuse Prevention

Kieran Sawyer, SSND & Kathie Amidei

ave maria press AmP notre dame, indiana

Nihil Obstat: Reverend Don Hying
                  Censor liborum

Imprimatur: The Most Reverend Timothy M. Dolan
                  Archbishop of Milwaukee

Given at Milwaukee, WI on 5 May 2006

The *Nihil Obstat* and *Imprimatur* are official declarations that a book or pamphlet is free of doctrinal or moral error. No implication is contained therein that those who have granted the *Nihil Obstat* or *Imprimatur* agree with its contents, opinions, or statements expressed.

Scripture texts in this work are cited with each reference.

Founded in 1865, Ave Maria Press is a ministry of the Indiana Province of Holy Cross.

www.avemariapress.com

ISBN-10 1-59471-088-0 ISBN-13 978-1-59471-088-9

Cover and text design by David Scholtes

Cover photo ©Royalty-Free/Corbis

Printed and bound in the United States of America.

This book is dedicated to all children everywhere and to the adults who love them, who want to help them develop warm and loving relationships, and who want to protect them from abuse of every kind.

Contents

Preface

In response to the crisis of sexual abuse of children and young people by some priests and bishops, the United States Conference of Catholic Bishops issued *Promise to Protect, Pledge to Heal: The Charter for the Protection of Children and Young People* (2003). This document states:

> Dioceses/eparchies will establish "safe environment" programs. They will cooperate with civil authorities, educators, and community organizations to provide education and training for children, youth, parents, ministers, educators and others about ways to make and maintain a safe environment for children. (Article 12)

Dioceses across the country grappled with the mandate to implement sexual abuse prevention programs in parish religious education and Catholic school settings. The first stage was the training of parish and Catholic school staffs in sexual abuse prevention awareness. While this was a challenging task, remarkable strides were made in a very short period of time.

The second stage, implementation of sexual abuse prevention curriculum for children, youth, and parents, proved more complex and far more challenging. It soon became clear that the available resources and approaches were far from adequate. This was especially true in the religious education setting, with its largely volunteer staff and significant time restrictions.

Parish and school leaders were genuinely concerned about the issue of child sexual abuse and eager to take any measures necessary to protect young people. Parents wanted to discuss this important topic with their children, but felt they did not have the information, resources, or expertise to initiate such conversations. Catechetical leaders in dioceses, parishes, and schools, faced with the mandate to present such sensitive material as part of the religious education program, were deeply concerned about how to integrate the material into the curriculum in an appropriate way. They worried about their own lack of training on the topic, and more so, their inability to prepare their classroom teachers and volunteer catechists for this daunting task.

It was out of these concerns that the *Learning about LIFE* program began. The program is based on three controlling principles:

- that any teaching on sexual abuse should be looked at in the wider context of positive, loving relationships;

- that any teaching on sexuality, positive or negative, should involve the parents working with their own children; and

- that the teaching on sexuality should be permeated with faith and rooted in the moral teachings of the Church.[1]

In our many dialogues with catechists and parents, we have discovered that parents welcomed the Church's invitation to educate their children in ways that would help to change the tragic reality of child sexual abuse and create a safer environment for their children. We learned that catechetical leaders wanted to partner with parents and the larger Church to be part of the solution to the crisis of child sexual abuse in our society. Parents are most willing to participate in programs to change the environment from one in which the sexual abuse of children can exist to one in which every child is safe to grow as a loving person. It was out of our discussions with catechists and parents that we have developed a family-based program that presents sexual abuse in the context of loving relationships and that allows parents to participate in awareness-raising sessions with their children and adolescents.

Sr. Kieran Sawyer, SSND
Kathie Amidei
January 2006

---

1. These principles are in harmony with the *National Directory for Catechesis* (2005), which calls for catechesis that "includes instruction on the gift of human sexuality, its inherent goodness, and the proper place of that gift within the context of a faithful, fruitful, and lifelong marriage."

Introduction

Protecting Our Children from Sexual Abuse

Children, by virtue of being children, have to trust the adults around them for the necessities of life they need for survival. Tragically, some disturbed adults will take advantage of that vulnerability and abuse children in many ways, including sexual abuse. Children are especially vulnerable to sexual abuse because they are physically small, intellectually immature, and lacking in the information that might help them to know how to protect themselves against someone who wishes them harm. The less informed a child is, the more vulnerable he or she is when faced with exploitation or abuse of any kind.

Caring adults can help to prevent sexual abuse by establishing a safe environment for their children. The way to do this includes:

- Limiting access to the children to those who need to have contact with them.

- Requiring criminal background checks for those who do have contact with the children.

- Participating in and advocating for awareness training for all adults in the children's lives.

- Learning to recognize the signs of those who might wish the children harm by sexually exploiting them.

Additionally, caring adults can prepare children to protect themselves against possible sexual exploitation, should it ever become necessary. We can prepare them in these ways by:

- Loving, supporting, and helping children to grow in self-esteem as the unique individual persons they are.

- Teaching children that their bodies are a sacred gift from God. Children need to know, from a young age, that their bodies have parts that are private and special and that only a few special adults (e.g., parents or doctors) should touch or see those private, special parts of their bodies when it is appropriate to keep them clean and safe.

- Giving children information about the possibility that older, bigger people might wish to harm them sexually.

- Teaching children that if they feel uncomfortable about the way any adult or bigger person interacts with them, they should say no, get away, ask for help, and keep asking until someone helps them.

Caring adults would prefer not to have to talk with children about this subject and often find themselves overwhelmed with sadness that such a discussion is necessary. But the truth is that children have often been victims of sexual abuse in the past and continue to be such. If adults can teach them to protect themselves, isn't it our responsibility to do so? Knowledge about sexual abuse prevention is basic safety information. We teach children that matches can burn them, seat belts can protect them, and looking both ways when they cross the street can keep them out of harm's way. In the same way, we should teach children how to recognize the signs that someone would wish to sexually exploit them and the strategies to protect themselves should they find themselves in this situation.

This mission, to create a safer world for our children, is the work of all caring adults. It is everyone's job. Certain people have a special responsibility to children. This program has been developed from the moral and doctrinal teachings of the Church to invite two of those groups, **parents** and **catechetical leaders**, to do just that by using the catechetical setting to empower parents to have these important conversations with their children in a way that is appropriate, comfortable, and helpful. These conversations, begun in the parish or school setting, will hopefully continue in the home. This program has been created to initiate these discussions in a setting of a faith community where parents can be given opportunities through discussion and activities to begin this important dialogue in their families.

The basic framework of these sessions is a gradual understanding by the children of the difference between the four kinds of human relationships represented by the acronym LIFE—Love, Infatuation, Friendship, and Exploitation. The distinction between these kinds of relationships is woven consistently throughout the program in age-appropriate ways. The reality of sexual abuse is presented in this context as a severe form of exploitation. It is pertinent to note that *Deus Caritas Est*, the first encyclical of Pope Benedict XVI, also speaks of human relationships in these four categories. The Holy Father uses the Greek words agape, eros, and filia to name three positive relationships and refers to the experience we are calling exploitation as a form of relationship that is "debased" and "deceptive," that is, it uses sex as a mere "commodity to be used and exploited."

It is the intention of the program to base the lesson about remaining safe and avoiding abuse in the context of teaching children that most relationships and interactions are loving and friendly. Most adults in children's lives should, and usually do, care for and protect them. At the same time, the program teaches children that sometimes people who are bigger or older might relate to them in ways that can make them feel uncomfortable or hurt them.

From a faith perspective, it is important to establish this discussion in a theology of the sacred trust of relationships, especially those relationships that protect the vulnerable.

The sessions are also based in the foundational teachings of the sacredness of one's body as a gift from God and a temple of the Holy Spirit. Having to teach our children to protect themselves from abuse, while it is an unfortunate reality, actually offers an opportunity for parishes, schools, and families to have important discussions about the foundational moral principles on which the Church's ethic of sexuality is based; that is, in the sacred gifts of life, of our bodies, and the relationships of intimacy that we will develop in our lives.

Finally, we hope these family discussions will be opportunities to learn more deeply that all of family life is rooted in gospel values—to protect the vulnerable, to respect those who cannot fully protect themselves, and to teach, protect and guard the dignity of each human being. We are created by God—body, mind, and soul—for eternity. We need to care for ourselves and each other because we are made in the image of God and created to learn to love.

Program Components

The program consists of six family-based sessions, one each for families with children in preschool, grades 1–2, grades 3–4, grades 5–6, grades 7–8, and grades 9–10. The program envisions gatherings of the children of the particular grade level with their parents in the school cafeteria or parish hall for sessions of one to two hours, depending of the age of the children. The director of the sessions leads the families in activities that help them to discuss positive loving relationships and sexuality as well as various forms of abusive relationships.

In the **preschool and grades 1–2 sessions**, all presentation of sensitive sexual content is done by the individual parents to their own children, following a process and handouts explained by the program director. The focus of these sessions is helping the children to realize that their bodies are gifts from God to be loved and protected, to realize that some parts of their bodies are private and special, and to understand that there are some adults or older youth who might not love and protect them.

The **grades 3–4 session** has the family work together to name what is special about their family and the individual members in it. Under the guidance of the director, the parents then tell their children about various types of abuse—physical, emotional, and sexual—and how to protect themselves from abuse. An activity on bullying follows. The families then create a small banner meant to remind them as a family to respect themselves and each other.

The **grades 5–6 session** begins with the family groupings doing fun activities that introduce the four kinds of relationships: Love, Infatuation, Friendship, and Exploitation. The children then come to the front of the room for a presentation by the director of the sensitive material concerning sexual abuse, and return to the family groupings to review the material with their parents. They then create a poster containing "The Big Three" rules: Say no. Get away. Tell someone you trust.

The **grades 7–8 and grades 9–10 sessions** begin with groups of three or four adolescents with their parents doing some director-led discussion of the four kinds of relationships. This is followed by presentations by the director to the teens, with their parents listening in the background, concerning the developing role of sexual relationships in their lives. Besides warning the young people about possible perpetrators of sexual abuse, these presentations show how the teens themselves can sometimes become involved in sexual activities that are exploitative and abusive.[2]

All of the activities at all levels are conducted in an atmosphere of respect, joy, seriousness, and family involvement. All include scriptural readings, prayer, and blessings of the children by their parents.

Special Roles for Conducting the Program

Though the primary catechesis of the program is shared from parent to child, there are several other adults who take on special roles in supporting the program. Some of the main roles are:

Pastor

The role of the pastor is to endorse the program and to explain to his parishioners the importance of talking to their children about sexuality, including the sad reality of sexual abuse. He emphasizes the importance of doing this in family units and in a context of loving relationships. The pastor encourages the parents to bring their children to each of the various age-level sessions. His own presence at these sessions will help to encourage the session directors and validate their message.

---

2. Additional activities for older adolescents, also based on LIFE concepts, can be found in *Sex and the Teenager* by Sr. Kieran Sawyer and published by Ave Maria Press.

Principal, Director of Religious Education, Youth Minister

The role of the principal and catechetical leaders is to create the structures that make the program possible. They recruit and prepare program directors for the various sessions, put the sessions on the calendar, send out announcements, invitations and permission letters, (see Sample Parent Letter, page 16), and provide hospitality for the meetings. They are also responsible for the mandatory reporting of any evidence of sexual abuse that might be surfaced through the program.

Program Director(s)

Each session is to be carefully prepared and presented by a program director (or team of directors). This person may be the DRE, a teacher, or catechist. The directors prepare the teaching charts, run off handouts, arrange the room, provide for nametags, gather all materials needed for the session, explain and guide the small group activities, and present the content in a comfortable and engaging manner. The importance of studying the manual until they are thoroughly at ease with the content and feel well prepared for each session cannot be overemphasized.

Teachers and Catechists

The regular classroom teachers and/or catechists help to disseminate promotional material, collect permission letters, and encourage their students to attend the family sessions. Ideally they themselves attend and participate in the sessions, to show their support, to become informed, and to be prepared to do follow-up in their classes by answering questions or giving further information.

Parents

Parents have the primary responsibility for providing their children with developing information on sexuality and for protecting them from abuse. The *Learning about LIFE* program is designed to help them fulfill this obligation. It is their responsibility to participate in all of the age-appropriate sessions with each child in their family and to be prepared to answer any questions their child(ren) might ask after the sessions.

Settings

The sessions described in this program should take place in a large room, like a church hall, gym, or school cafeteria, with moveable chairs and the proper acoustics so that everyone can clearly hear the presentations. Space should be provided for both small-group and large-group settings. Large-group settings are also used for games and for prayer.

For the lower–grade programs (through grade 6), each family grouping should be seated at a separate table, or at the opposite ends of long cafeteria-type tables. In the lower grades, all sensitive content is presented by parents to their children.

For the middle and upper grade programs, small groupings of six to nine should be made up of three adolescents with their parents. After introductory activities in their small groups, the teens are gathered at the front of the space, close to the director, who presents the sensitive content of the session. The parents, sitting behind them, are given the main points of the presentation on a handout sheet, which they use later to review the content with their own children.

Teaching Charts

The director's presentation of sensitive material is guided by the use of teaching charts. Key points of the lesson are outlined on 8 1/2" x 11" sheets of heavy paper or on overhead transparencies. When paper charts are used, the director gathers the children close to him/herself, and sits, holding the charts on his/her lap, where the children can easily see them. The director then speaks seriously and intimately to the children, showing each card and explaining it. For the older children, parts of the session also require the use of a whiteboard, chalkboard or larger chart. Developing a transparency presentation using the teaching charts is also an option.

The content of the teaching charts is included at the end of each session, designed as separate transparencies. The actual teaching charts are available as PDF files online at http://www.avemariapress.com/itemdetail.cfm?nItemid=790. These can be reproduced as charts or developed as overheads for presentation.

Dear Parents,

The problem of child sexual abuse is a concern of the Catholic Church as well as our society in general. This crisis offers an opportunity to improve our ability to discuss, as families, the important topic of relationships that enrich our lives and those which could harm us or cause harm to others.

We would like to invite your family to a session to address the issue of sexual abuse in the context of learning more about healthy and unhealthy relationships. The content of the session will help you as parents to discuss with your children relationships that are loving and friendly as compared to relationships that are harmful. With your children, you will consider ways people relate to each other, develop skills to better recognize and understand feelings, and learn ways to ask for help should they not feel safe at any time or in any way.

The program for children in grades _____ will be held:

Date: _____

Time: _____

Place: _____

It is obligatory that parents attend this session with their children.

As members of this faith community, we hope to partner with parents in giving our children the information they would need if they were in danger of being harmed, so they can assist in their own self-protection. Together we can work toward minimizing the risk of all child abuse, especially child sexual abuse.

Please call if you have any questions or concerns regarding this program or its content.

Sincerely,

Learning about

L I F E

---

for Children in Preschool

and Kindergarten and Their Parents

Session Introduction

This is the preschool and kindergarten session of a program designed to help parents and children to discuss some basic concepts concerning the relationships that spell the acronym LIFE (Love, Infatuation, Friendship, and Exploitation). Because of the age of the children, this session will present only the concepts of Love and Friendship in simplified terms. (The full acronym is introduced to parents.) The concept of sexual abuse is presented in this context.

The session begins with a song that praises God for creating us, body, mind and soul, and reminds the children that each person is special. Then a large group game is played, similar to "Simon Says," called "God Created Me to Do This, God Created Me To Do That." This game presents a way that is fun to use our bodies.

Next the children are presented with the concept that one way we use our bodies is to communicate with one another. Some communications feel good, like a "high five" from a friend, and some communications don't feel good, like being pushed. Because we are all God's children, and all are created good, it is important to treat everyone with respect. We should only touch others' bodies, and expect our bodies to be touched, in ways that don't make us feel hurt or confused.

Parents are then given an opportunity to do work on an activity book with their children. It is called *Learning To Love God's Creation*. The session ends with a closing prayer service based on Jesus blessing the children (Matthew 19:13–15). Parents then pray a blessing for their own children.

Who This Session Is For

Children in preschool (age four) through kindergarten with their parents

Goals

- To support children in establishing their identity as children of God as well as individuals in their own families.

- To help parents and children discuss relationships that are loving and friendly and identify other experiences that might be harmful to a child

- To teach children that they should feel safe with others and how to ask for help if they don't feel safe.

- To teach children that people who love them or are friends to them will not treat them in ways that make them feel afraid or uncomfortable.

- To tell children that their bodies have parts that are private and special.

- To establish an understanding with the children that no one, except certain people under certain circumstances, should touch those special and private body parts. With parents' guidance, children will consider what those circumstances should be.

Materials

- whiteboard or chalkboard

- stapler

- markers or crayons (one pack for each child)

- pencils (one for each child)

- construction paper for paper hearts

- scissors

- glue

- yarn

- hole puncher

Preparations

- Prepare a transparency or a chart with the words to the "Body, Mind, and Soul" song (page 37) and online at www.avemariapress.com.

- Duplicate, assemble, and staple the *Learning To Love God's Creation Activity Books*, page 28 (one copy for each child).

- Duplicate the *Parent Prayer* handout, page 35 (one for each family).

- Use the heart pattern on page 36 for tracing hearts on construction paper. Cut out hearts (one for each child). Also, make copies of the *Parent Blessing Prayer* (one for each child) and cut out each heart. Glue the *Parent Prayer Blessing* to the construction paper heart. Punch a hole at the top of the heart. Thread with yarn (approximately 18") to make a necklace.

Parent Prayer Blessing on the back:

Parent Blessing Prayer:

You are a child of God and a child
of mine.
God loves you. I love you.
I ask our God the Father to protect
you from all harm.
I ask Jesus our brother to bless you
with a kind heart.
I ask the Spirit of God to be with
you always in all you do.
Amen.

Preschool/Kindergarten Lesson Plan

A. Opening

Gather as a large group with parents and children seated together as a family, at tables. Allow enough space that each parent can talk quietly with his or her own child(ren).

1. *Welcome everyone. Tell them:*

> Welcome, parents and children, to this session. You are going to talk about some things that are important and that you will need to know and remember. First, we will talk about how God made you with a wonderful body, mind, and soul. We will especially think about your wonderful body that God created and about some ways to keep it safe and happy.

2. *Say to the parents:*

> Parents, this is the first lesson in a program that teaches about **LIFE** That is an acronym for **L**ove, **I**nfatuation, **F**riendship, and **E**xploitation (write on the board). The purpose of this program is to help us to teach our children that we should relate to others in ways that are loving and friendly. The adults in our children's lives should, and usually do, care for and protect them. But it is also important to be aware that it is rare but possible that sometimes people who are older and bigger than they are can relate to them in ways that can make children feel uncomfortable or hurt them. It is hoped that this session will be an opportunity for you and your child to have a conversation about this important topic.

> This session will be an opportunity for you to reflect on God's gift of your children to you. It will encourage you to express your love to your children and remind them that your love expresses God's love. Together we will thank God for the gift of our whole beings: bodies, minds, and souls. We will establish some ways we relate to each other in friendship and love through our bodies. You also will have a chance to tell your children what parts of their bodies are private and special. Finally, you will discuss the ways children need to learn to protect themselves from someone who might hurt them by touching them in inappropriate ways.

3. *Address the children. Say to them:*

> Boys and girls, we are happy you are here together with your mom or dad. We are going to talk about someone special. Do you know who that might be? (Accept answers.) It is you! We are going to sing a song and play a game together. Then your mom and/or dad will do an activity book with you called *Learning To Love God's Creation*. In our time together, we will talk about a very special gift from God, your body. We will tell you about one way to keep your body safe.

B. Song

Ask everyone to stand.

1. *Tell the parents and children:*

> You are going to sing a song. Singing is one way to pray and praise God. We are going to praise God because we are so happy that he made us

Hold up the chart or display a transparency with the words to the "Body, Mind, and Soul" song (page 37). Some children may be able to read them.

2. *Tell the children:*

> This is a simple song, and you will learn it from reading the words or by listening to it.

Say the words to each line of the song. Ask the group, parents and children, to repeat each line after you. Point to them each time it is their turn to say a line.

> I am special.
>
> You are special.
>
> Created by God.
>
> Created by God.
>
> Body, mind, and soul.
>
> God made them all.
>
> Praise the Lord!
>
> Praise the Lord!

Repeat a second time reciting two lines at a time.

Sing each line to the song using the tune "Frère Jacque." Have the group repeat each line after you. Finally, have the group sing the song all the way through together. Have the group clap in appreciation for this wonderful expression of praise to God!

C. Large-Group Game

Ask the parents to sit down and the children to gather in an open space.

1. *Give the parents a paper heart for their child already threaded with yarn. Tell them:*

> Write your child's name on the front of the heart and put it on the prayer table when finished. Then you can return to the open space and watch your children play a game.

2. *When the children have gathered in a space open enough to play the game, tell them:*

> You are going to play a little game called "God Created Me to Do This, God Created Me to Do That" that will use your body in a good way. It is a game like "Simon Says."

The leader stands or sits where all the children can see him or her. The leader will do an action, and as the action is demonstrated tell the children the leader will say either:

> "God created me to do this" or "God created me to do that."

The children should only repeat the action when the leader says, "God created me to do this" as the action is done. If the leader does an action and says "God created me to do that" the children should not repeat the action. If they do repeat the action when the leader says "God created me to do that," that child will have to sit down, as in "Simon Says."

Some actions that might be used are: waving a hand, holding a finger to an ear, clapping, hopping, jumping in place, stamping feet, skipping once or twice, flapping arms, standing on one foot, tapping shoulders, giving a thumbs up sign, turning around in a circle, running in place. The game may be led by the group leader or by a willing parent. Play the game for a few minutes, doing at least two rounds, so children who were eliminated early have a chance to play a second time.

After playing the game, have the children return to the tables with their families.

3. *Remind the children:*

> This was a happy and fun way to use your own bodies. There are also actions *between* people that use our bodies in ways that feel good.

4. *Ask the children and parents:*

> What are some of those actions? (Accept reasonable answers like, shaking hands, a hug from someone who loves us, a pat on the back, a high five, etc.)

5. *Tell them:*

> There are ways people use their bodies that hurt people or don't feel good to people.

6. *Ask:*

> What are some ways to use our bodies in actions between people that do not feel good? (Accept reasonable answers like hitting, punching, pushing, etc.)

7. *Say:*

> As the song and game said, it is God who creates all of us. Because we are part of the human family, we all are children of God and it is very important that we all use our bodies and touch each other in good ways that make others and ourselves feel comfortable. We should expect others to treat us in the same good ways and not touch us in ways that hurt us or make us feel bad or confused.

Tell them they will now have an opportunity to do an activity book with their parents that is called *Learning to Love God's Creation*. When they have finished, they will talk about their work.

D. Activity Book

Pass out the activity books that are made by reproducing the *Learning to Love God's Creation* activity book pages and stapling the pages together (see pages 28–35). Make a book for each child. If there is more than one child per family, each child should have his or her own book. Also give a pencil and a pack of crayons or markers to each child.

1. *Say to the parents:*

> Parents, this section of the program is done between you and your child so that each parent can pace this discussion, as you believe is appropriate for your child.

> Work through the pages in the activity book with your child. Help your child as needed. For example, write your child's name, if assistance

is needed, but allow your child to do as much as possible, with you coaching them, reading to them as needed, and affirming their correct answers and their effort. Work at a pace that is comfortable for your child.

Parents, this is your opportunity to say what you would like your child to know about protecting themselves from sexual abuse. For instance, discuss who to ask for help if someone touches them in a way that makes them feel uncomfortable or hurts them. Practice with your child how to ask for help.

Allow time for each family to work on the activity book.

E. Closing Prayer Service

After everyone has had an opportunity to complete the activity book, gather the entire group, parents and children, to stand in a large circle. Ask the parents to stand behind their child and put their hands on their child's shoulders.

1. *Say to families:*

Thank you for participating in this important session. We hope you learned something important about God's wonderful creation, YOU! We hope you remember how important it is to keep yourselves safe. God wants you to be safe, well cared for, and to live a happy life with others. All children should have many people to love them and care for them. God wants you to have friends and to be a good friend to others. It is never right to hurt another person. We must always try to respect other people and to expect other people to respect us, including our bodies.

Now we will close our session with a little prayer blessing the children who are here.

2. *Retrieve hearts.*

Have the parents retrieve the hearts they made from the prayer table. (Do not give them to the children yet.) Choose a parent to do a scripture reading as part of the closing prayer service.

3. *Sign of the Cross.*

Lead the group in the Sign of the Cross.

4. *Scripture Reading.*

Call on the parent reader to proclaim the gospel passage of the blessing of the children from Matthew 19:13–15.

5. *Offer a short reflection on the scripture reading and a chance for the parents to bless their children. Say:*

> Remember boys and girls, Jesus loves you as his own child. Never hesitate to ask Jesus for whatever you need. You are a child of God. Your parents also love you. Never hesitate to ask them for what you need. You are a beloved child to your mom and dad. Now your parents are going to give you a sign of their love and God's love.

> Parents, please take your heart necklace, stand in front of your child, and read the prayer to him/her. Then place the necklace over your child's head.

> You are a child of God and a child of mine.

> God loves you. I love you.

> I ask our God the Father to protect you from all harm.

> I ask Jesus, our brother, to bless you with a kind heart.

> I ask the Spirit of God to be with you always in all you do.

> Amen.

When all are back in place, invite the parents and children to share a sign of peace and love. Thank everyone for coming.

LEARNING TO LOVE GOD'S CREATION

God created a wonderful world.

Color the picture of God's creation.

One of God's most precious creations is YOU!

My name is:

_____

Draw a picture of yourself.

You are a child of God.

People who love you and who are a friend to you
will care for you and protect you.

God made you with a mind to learn and think and a soul to know and love God, yourself, and others. Your soul will live forever. God gave you a body so you can do great things with the gift of your life.

God created your body with legs to run and jump and hands to draw and play.

The grown-ups in your life care and
protect you in many ways, including helping to
care for your body.

In the picture frames,
name or draw the
grown-ups who care for
you and protect you.

Certain parts of your body, the private parts, need special protection and care. Only a few people have permission to see or touch the special and private parts of a child's body, like parents who bathe their child's body to keep it clean, or the doctor who is giving someone medical attention.

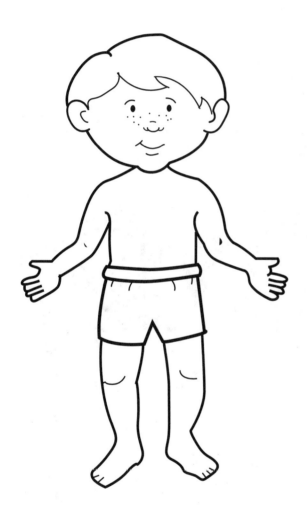

Color the special private parts of our bodies. They are the parts covered by a bathing suit.

If a grown-up or an older child asks you to take off your clothes or touches your private parts in a way that makes you feel uncomfortable or bad, ask for help from someone you trust.

There are three important rules to remember if this should ever happen to you:

1. Say no.

2. Get away.

3. Tell someone you trust.

(Keep telling until someone helps you.)

Trace the letters in the words of the Big Three Rules.

God and all the people who love you want you to be safe and happy. That is why it is important to care for and protect your whole body, including the special private parts of your body. Think of something you like to do that uses the gift of your body. Draw a picture of you doing that.

Make up a little prayer that you or your mom or dad
writes on this page, thanking God for creating you and
giving you such a wonderful body!

Dear God,

Thank you for _____

_____.

I will care for your creation by _____

_____.

I like that you made me _____

_____.

Love,

_____

Parent Blessing Prayer:

You are a child of God and a child
of mine.
God loves you. I love you.
I ask our God the Father to protect
you from all harm.
I ask Jesus our brother to bless you
with a kind heart.
I ask the Spirit of God to be with
you always in all you do.
Amen.

Body, Mind, and Soul

I am special.

You are special.

Created by God.

Created by God.

Body, mind, and soul.

God made them all.

Praise the Lord!

Praise the Lord!

Learning about
LIFE

Learning about

L I F E

for Children in Grades 1 and 2 and Their Parents

Session Introduction

This is the grade 1–2 session of a program designed to help parents and children to discuss some basic concepts concerning the relationships that spell the acronym LIFE (Love, Infatuation, Friendship, and Exploitation). Because of the age of the children, this session will present only the concepts of Love, Friendship, and Exploitation in simplified terms. (The full acronym is introduced to parents.) The concept of sexual abuse is presented in the context of exploitation.

In the opening activity, the children and parents are welcomed. The parents are introduced to the LIFE acronym. The children are asked to list some people in their lives who love and protect them and individuals who are friends to them. The families then do an activity from the *Me, Lovable Me* handout together at a table.

This is followed by a large-group activity where ways to show or not show love are considered. Families are then invited to discuss among themselves appropriate ways to show love and friendship with their bodies. This activity includes a discussion about the private and special parts of their bodies and how they should be treated.

As a large-group summary, the children will practice asking for help if someone touches them in a way that makes them feel uncomfortable or confused. The children are introduced to the "Big Three Rules": Say No. Get Away. Tell Someone you trust.

As a large group, they will play a life-size game of Tic-Tac-Toe that reviews the material that was presented in the lesson.

The session ends with parents helping their children to complete a prayer that is used in the closing prayer service. The prayer service focuses on the story of the Lost Sheep (Matthew 18: 10–14), reminding the children how important it is to God that they are safe and loved.

Who this Session Is For

For children in grades 1 and 2 with their parents

Goals

- To help parents and children discuss relationships and experiences with others that are loving and friendly and to encourage them to recognize their value as children of God.

- To help parents and children discuss experiences that can make a child feel uncomfortable and fearful or that can hurt them.

- To teach children that they should feel safe with others and ask for help if they don't. People who love them or are a friend to them should not touch them or talk to them in ways that make them feel afraid or uncomfortable.

- To establish with the children that their body, mind, and spirit are precious gifts from God. Parents and the adults who care for them should protect the children's body, mind, and spirit.

- To tell children that their bodies have parts that are private and special.

- To introduce to the parents the terms discussed in this program— Love, Infatuation, Friendship and Exploitation.

Materials

pens, pencils, markers, or crayons (one set for each child)

newsprint, white-board, or chalkboard

construction paper

scissors

cotton balls

glue (one for every two or three families)

Preparations

- Prepare a transparency or print the LIFE chart (page 54) on newsprint or a board.

- Duplicate the *Private and Special Parts of Our Bodies* handout, page 48 (one for each child).

- Duplicate the *Me, Lovable Me* handout, page 50 (one for each child).

- Prepare a transparency or print the Goals of the Session (page 55) on newsprint or a board.

- Prepare a transparency or print the *Big Three Rules* chart (page 56) on newsprint or a board.

- Cut out large X's and O's for the Tic-Tac-Toe game from construction paper.

- For the Tic-Tac-Toe game, arrange nine chairs in rows 3 x 3.

- Use the sheep pattern on page 51 to cut out sheep from construction paper (one for each child).

- Duplicate *A Child's Prayer* handout on page 52 (one for each child).

Grades 1 and 2 Lesson Plan

A. Opening

Gather as a large group, preferably sitting at tables with chairs, each family sitting together. More than one family can be seated at a table but each family should be seated so the family can talk with one another, preferably with some degree of privacy.

1. *Welcome the children and parents who are gathered for the session. Say to them:*

> Welcome to this session. We are going to focus your time together on a great gift that God has given us, to be a human person with a body, mind, and spirit. Each person is special and loved by God. Because each of us is a beloved child of God, we are given the important responsibility to protect each other. Grown-ups have a special responsibility to protect children so that each person has a chance to grow up in a safe environment, learning to love and be loved.

2. *Say to parents:*

> Parents, this is one session of a program that teaches about **LIFE**, an acronym for **Love, Infatuation, Friendship,** and **Exploitation** (refer to the chart or transparency or print on the board). The purpose of this program is to help us to work together as faith communities and as families to teach our children to recognize relationships with others that are loving, friendly, and healthy. It also is important to teach our children to recognize relationships that are dangerous or uncomfortable to us and to learn ways to get out of such encounters. Grown-ups like parents, teachers, priests, and leaders in schools, parishes, and our community are supposed to protect children. The

goal of this session is to give children and parents information about this aspect of life, language to discuss it, and strategies to deal with situations if a child does not feel safe or comfortable.

3. *Say to children:*

> Boys and girls, we are happy to be here together with you and your parents to discuss an important subject: YOU! You are a special person. God has given you a wonderful body. God loves you very much! Your parents love you very much! Do you know who else loves you? (Listen to their answers one at a time, with the large group; for example, grandma, grandpa, brothers, sisters, God, etc.)

4. *Then ask:*

> Who is a friend to you? (Listen to their answers: neighbors, classmates, parents of their friends, Jesus, etc.)

5. *Finally, ask them:*

> Who do you think should protect you? (Listen to their answers: parents, bus drivers, police, teachers, etc.)

Thank them for their answers.

6. *Conclude by explaining the following. Say:*

> In this session we are going to discuss (write these goals on the board or newsprint or use the transparency on page 55.)

- **How special you are as a child of God**

- **Who loves you**

- **Who is a friend to you**

- **How important it is that you, as a child, are protected so you can grow up in safety and be loved.**

B. Family Activity

Distribute pens, markers, and crayons to each table (one set per family). Give the *Me, Lovable Me* handout on page 50 to each family and tell the parents to complete the sheet with their children. Parents should do a separate sheet for each child if they have more than one child present.

C. Large-Group Activity

When families have completed the handout, focus their attention in the large group.

1. *Prepare two columns on the board or newsprint.*

Label one column **Ways to Show Love or Friendship to a Child of God**. Label the other **Ways That Do Not Show Love or Friendship to a Child of God**.

2. *Begin the activity.*

First, ask a child to give a suggestion for one of the columns. Then ask a parent to give a suggestion. Continue to accept answers and list them on the newsprint until you think you have an adequate representation of answers in each column. For the first column, responses may include hugs, handshakes, making a meal, holding a hand, driving to school, taking walks, joking, and the like. For the second column, responses may include things like shaking, hitting, pushing, hugs that are too hard.

D. Family Discussion

When you have completed the large-group activity, have them focus as individual families.

1. *Tell them:*

> We are going to discuss an important topic as individual families. Parents, you now will have an opportunity to discuss for a few minutes with your own children the many good ways we show love through our bodies. For example, like through a good hug a parent gives a child. Parents, you also can discuss what parts of our bodies are private and special. Finally, you can tell in age-appropriate language the ways a person should touch their bodies.

2. *Parent Discussion*

Give the handout *Private and Special Parts of Our Body* (pages 48-49) to parents and ask them to discuss the private parts of the body with their child(ren). Allow as much time as parents continue to discuss this handout with their family.

E. Large-Group Summary

When families have completed the discussion ask them to join together as a large group again.

1. *Say to the children:*

> We know that most people are friendly. Many people love and protect you. But it is important that children know that someone could have an experience that could make the person feel uncomfortable or hurt him or her. If that ever happens to you, there are many people who will protect you. But those people will only know to do so if you let adults you trust know that you need help.

Ask for volunteers who are willing to show the others how to ask for help. (Accept any reasonable response that is appropriate. For example, "Help!" or "Mom, I don't like the way Aunt Mary hugs me too tightly." Or simply run away or leave the room.) Offer suggestions if needed or ask parents to give examples if children don't.

2. *Continue talking with the children. Ready the display of the* Big Three Rules *on a transparency, newsprint, or the board. Say:*

> Touches should feel good. If someone touches you in a way that feels confusing, uncomfortable, or bad, it is very important that you tell that person to stop, even if that person is a grown-up and you are a child. Get help from someone else if that person does not stop.

> There are three very important rules to remember if you feel that someone touches you in a way that makes you feel bad, confused or uncomfortable.

Hold up the chart titled, *Big Three Rules*. Ask the children to read them out loud together with you.

- **SAY NO.**

- **GET AWAY.**

- **TELL SOMEONE YOU TRUST .**
  (KEEP TELLING UNTIL SOMEONE LISTENS.)

Ask if there are any questions about the rules. Discuss how they might say "No," and whom they might tell if they would need to get help by telling someone.

3. *Review the Big Three Rules. Say to the children*:

> If I hide the rules, who could stand up and say the first rule?

Hide the first rule and call on a child to stand up and tell you the first rule. Do the same with the second and third rule and then all three of the rules together.

D. Tic-Tac-Toe Game

Prepare to play a game of Tic-Tac-Toe. Set up nine chairs in three rows of three chairs each in a space all can see. Divide the group into two teams with parents and children on each team. Give each team several X's and O's cut from construction paper available.

1. *Play the game.*

Give each side an opportunity to answer the questions listed below. As they answer the questions correctly, they choose a representative from their team to pick a chair to sit in holding their X or O to try to win the game. Play until you have answered all the questions or the group loses interest. If one team wins and time permits, you can play subsequent rounds.

2. *Use the following Tic-Tac-Toe questions:*

For Children

- Who is the person who has the right to decide if a touch feels good or bad? ("Each person has the right to decide for themselves" or "I do!" Or accept a similar answer.)

- Name someone who is supposed to protect you. (Mom, Dad, doctors, nurses, police officers, and grandparents. This question can be asked several different times eliciting different answers.)

- Name something you are good at that you wrote in the figure in the *Me, Lovable Me* activity. (This question can be asked several times eliciting different answers from different children.)

- Give an example of a good touch between you and a grown-up friend. (Accept reasonable answers like a high five, a handshake, a pat on the back, etc. This question can be repeated.)

For Parents

- What does the **L** in the LIFE acronym stand for? (Love)

- What does the **I** in the LIFE acronym stand for? (Infatuation or in love)

- What does the **F** in the LIFE acronym stand for? (Friendship)

- What does the **E** in the LIFE acronym stand for? (Exploitation)

- Who is supposed to protect your child? (Accept reasonable answers like "I am," "teachers," "police officers.")

- Who should your child tell if they do not like the way someone touches them? (Parents and other trusted adults. This question can be repeated.)

- Give an example of a touch that is good between you and your child. (Accept reasonable answers, for example, a hug, a back rub, or a kiss. This question can be repeated.)

E. Prayer Activity

Pass out the handout *A Child's Prayer* (page 52) and a pack of crayons to each family.

1. *Tell the parents and children:*

> As a family, fill in the blanks on the *A Child's Prayer* handout. You will be writing a prayer that you can bring home after this session to say together at bedtime.

> Parents, allow your child to write as much of this as they can themselves. Help them as needed. Try to use as much of your child's own words even if you are recording them. Children, draw a picture on the sheet of someone who loves and protects you.

F. Closing Prayer

Close the evening by having parents and children gather together for a closing prayer.

1. *Introduce the prayer. Say:*

> We are going to read a short story from the Bible that will give us a picture of who God is and also remind us of how God wants us to be protected.

2. *Scripture Reading*

Call on one of the parents to read Matthew 18:10–14, the parable of the Lost Sheep.

3. *Sheep Cut-out*

After the scripture reading, give each child a sheep cut-out. Have them work with their parents to glue some cotton balls on the sheep.

4. *A Child's Prayer. When they have finished gluing cotton on the sheep, say:*

Take this little sheep home and keep it to remind you how important it is to God that you are safe and loved.

Let us close our session together by having each family individually pray *A Child's Prayer* that you wrote together.

Thank everyone for coming.

PRIVATE AND SPECIAL PARTS OF OUR BODIES

Parents:

In your family group, have a discussion with your child about the private parts of a person's body. Adjust your conversation to the age, experience, and comfort level of you and your child. You may want to include the following points:

- God created us as persons with bodies. That is good. We are made in the image and likeness of God.

- Jesus came to be with us as a human being with a body to teach us how sacred our human life is.

- To respect the gift of life, it is necessary to protect the body. Keep it clean, healthy, and safe. It is up to the responsible grown-ups in a child's life, the bigger society, and the child himself or herself to protect a child and make sure his or her body is treated with respect.

- There are parts of the human body that need special respect and protection. We call these our private and special body parts. Only a few people, under certain circumstances, should see or touch these private and special body parts. Give an example to your child that you, as a parent, feel is an appropriate person to touch these parts. For example, refer to your family doctor and remind your child of a recent doctor visit, and tell your child that is the work of a doctor to take care of the bodies of his or her patients and to keep them healthy. That might require a doctor needing to see or touch a person's private and special body parts.

- Continue this discussion until you believe your child understands and is clear about this concept.

- Finally, in the illustration, have your child color the private parts of a person's body. You can explain this by saying these are the parts covered by a bathing suit.

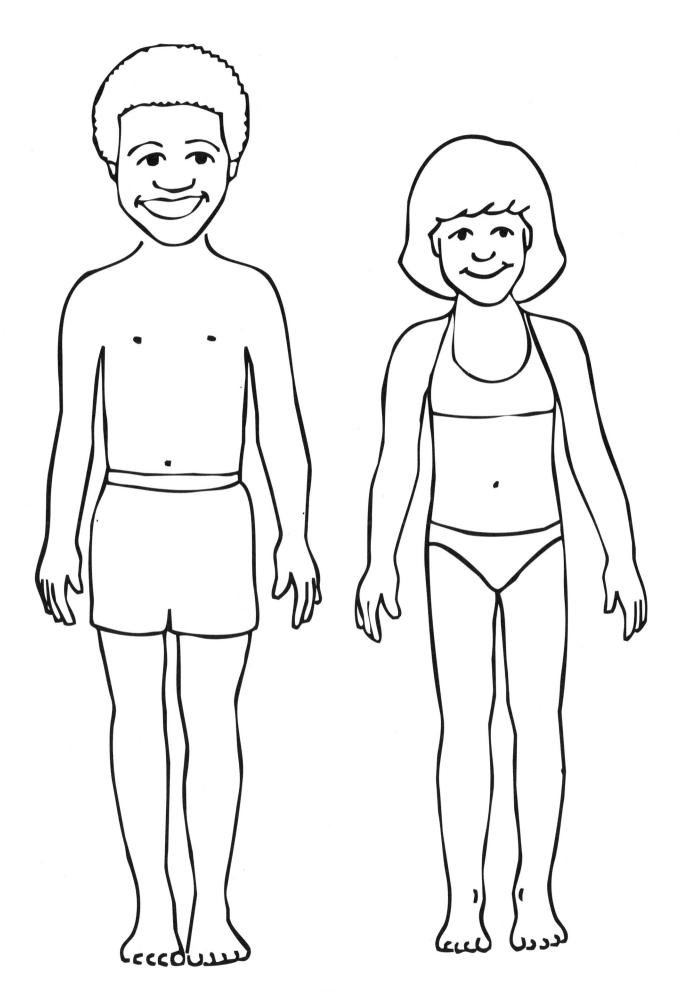

Me, Lovable Me!

God made you good!

God made you a wonderful person and gave you a beautiful body.

Don't ever forget how precious you are
and what a wonderful person
God created you to be!

Directions: Add hairstyle and other features to make the figure look like you. Then, write, or have your parents write, words that describe how you are good and what you are good at (for example, musical, kind, athletic). In the hearts, write the names of people you know who should protect you and whom you can ask for help if you feel afraid or uncomfortable (for example, grandparents, teachers, police officers).

A Child's Prayer

Thank you, God, for making me and for giving me this day.

Thank you for the name, _____ , that my parents gave me.

As I lay down to rest I think of the special way you made me.

I especially thank you for making my body so I can _____

_____

_____

_____, and

_____ .

I thank you for making my heart so I can _____

_____

_____ ,

And I thank you for making my soul so I can love you and always be close to you, my God.

Please keep grown-ups around me to protect and love me,

friends to play and talk with me

and a special angel to watch over me.

Amen.

Draw a picture of you and someone who loves and protects you.

LIFE Chart

Love

Infatuation

Friendship

Exploitation

Session Goals

You will be able to know:

- **How special you are as a child of God**

- **Who loves you**

- **Who is a friend to you**

- **How important it is that you, as a child, are protected so you can grow up in safety and be loved.**

Big Three Rules

- **SAY NO.**

- **GET AWAY.**

- **TELL SOMEONE YOU TRUST.**

  (KEEP TELLING UNTIL SOMEONE LISTENS.)

Learning about
L I F E

Learning about

L I F E

for Children in Grades 3 and 4 and Their Parents

Session Introduction

This is the grade 3–4 session of a program designed to help parents and children discuss some basic concepts concerning the relationships that spell the acronym L.I.F.E (Love, Infatuation, Friendship, and Exploitation). Because of the age of the children, this session will present only the concepts of Love, Friendship and Exploitation in simplified terms. (The full acronym is introduced to parents.) The concept of abuse is presented in the context of Exploitation.

Following an introduction to the session, there is a short prayer service focusing on Jesus' desire for us to show love and respect to others and ourselves (John 3:16–18). As a warm-up, each family completes a *Family Interview Sheet* and shares some of their answers with the large group.

Using the handout *Types of Abuse*, each family is given time to discuss what abuse is, the different forms abuse can take, and what to do to protect one's self from abuse. A short presentation on bullying, a type of abuse, is also shared.

Next, each family makes a *Respect Banner* as a reminder of the importance of respecting one's self and others. The concepts of abuse and respect are reviewed in a large group with the children doing an activity that allows them to evaluate ways a person might not be shown respect and care.

The session ends with the families reading together the Prayer of St. Francis.

Who This Session Is For

Children in grades 3 and 4 with their parents

Goals:

- To help parents and children discuss how they get along with other people in positive ways.

- To give parents and children an opportunity to discuss experiences that can make children feel uncomfortable and fearful, or that can hurt them.

- To give parents and children an opportunity to identify positive things about their families.

- To become aware of the issues of abuse.

- To learn what abuse entails and various ways that a child can be abused.

- To establish the importance of respect for one's self and respect for others.

- To help children identify whom to ask for help if they feel they are in an unsafe situation.

Materials

- 8" x 11" sheets of construction paper of different colors

- pens or pencils (one for each child)

- markers (one set for each child)

- scissors (one for each child)

- bibles (one per family)

- newsprint

Preparations

- Duplicate the *Family Interview* handout, page 67 (one for each family).

- Duplicate the *Types of Abuse* handout, pages 68–69 (one for each family).

- Duplicate the *Respect Banner* handout, page 71 (one for each family).

- Make three flash cards, one with the word **Abuse**, another with the word **Respect**, and a third with the word **Bullying**, each printed large enough for the group to see. These words may also be presented on a transparency (see page 73 online at www.avemariapress.com).

- Duplicate the handout *Abuse Scenarios*, pages 70 (one for each family).

- Prepare three signs, with one for each of the following words: **Physical Abuse**, **Emotional Abuse**, and **Sexual Abuse**.

- Duplicate the *Prayer of St. Francis* handout, page 72 (one for each family).

Grades 3 and 4 Lesson Plan

A. Opening

Gather family groups together at tables with children sitting with their parents. Space the groups to allow for some privacy. Begin by welcoming the families to the session.

1. *Say to the parents and children:*

> This session is part of a program that is called LIFE, an acronym for Love, Infatuation, Friendship, and Exploitation. Its purpose is to teach that relationships are an important part of life. Most relationships are good and healthy and part of God's plan for us to live together in families and communities. Unfortunately, there are some situations in life where we could be in a relationship or an experience where another person is trying to hurt or exploit us. It is important to learn to recognize those situations and to know how to ask for help if that ever occurs to us.

> We are gathering to talk about something all children should know. It is important that all children feel they are in a safe environment. If for any reason you, or any child you know, does not feel they are safe, it is important to learn to ask for help. At this session, you and your family will discuss this topic so that we know that each child here feels comfortable and safe in all situations in life. We will begin our session by praying together.

B. Prayer

Begin with the Sign of the Cross followed by the scripture reading.

1. *Scripture Reading*

Choose someone in the group to read 1 John 3:16–18, the need to love as Jesus did in deed and truth.

2. *Offer a short reflection on the reading. Say:*

Lord God, you bring us here together to learn more about how you created us and how you want us to live in peace and happiness with each other. We know that each person is precious to you.

You sent your Son, Jesus, to live in a family because you wanted him to have the chance to live life fully here on Earth. You gave Jesus his parents, other relatives, and friends to protect and guide him while he was a child. You want the same for us.

Open our minds to take this opportunity to better understand ourselves and the world around us. Teach us to love and protect each other in every way that we can. Keep us mindful of all the blessings of everyday life that we might take for granted, especially the gift of living in a family with each other.

Open our hearts to hear anew your unconditional love for us. We ask this through Christ Our Lord and the Holy Spirit. Amen.

3. *Conclude the prayer with the following discussion. Say to the parents and children:*

Jesus not only talked about love, he showed love in his actions. We, too, are called to not only talk about respect, love, and compassion, but also to treat each other in these ways. We should also expect others to treat us in these ways too.

What might be ways we show our respect, love, and compassion toward each other? (Possible answers might be: helping each other with physical needs like making a meal for someone or helping someone carry something heavy; saying things in ways that a person senses that we care about them; touching people respectfully, like shaking hands when we meet someone.)

Explain that all people and especially children should feel safe, physically and emotionally. It is the work of parents, teachers, and the whole community to make sure children are protected from persons who would not treat them as God wants them to be treated. Children must also learn how to recognize when they are not being treated with respect and how to get help when they need it.

C. Warm-up Exercise

Give each family a copy of the *Family Interview* handout (page 67). Ask them to discuss the sections and record their answers on the sheet. After each family has done that, call on representatives from several families (children and parents) to share some sample responses from the various sections.

D. Parent/Child Discussion of Types of Abuse

This discussion is the heart of the lesson, the chance for parents to share information about this topic with their child. Begin by giving each parent the handout *Types of Abuse* (pages 68–69).

1. *Say to parents and children:*

> Unfortunately, all children are not safe and protected as they should be. When people are not treated as they should be, we call this abuse. There are different ways children may not be protected or may possibly be hurt.

2. *Discussion*

Allow each family an opportunity to discuss the information in this handout on the level that is appropriate for the ages of their children. Invite the parents to record some of their child's responses to each question if they wish.

E. Bullying

Invite the children to come forward and sit on the floor near you. Invite their parents to move their chairs in close behind them.

1. *Say to the children:*

> Usually when we think of child abuse, we think of the bad things some adults do to children. Now I want to talk to you about a kind of abuse that some children do to other children. It is called "bullying." (Show flash card with the word "Bullying.") Like adult forms of child abuse, bullying might be physical, emotional, or sexual. Children act like bullies when they deliberately do mean things to other children. The child who is being bullied is hurt, frightened, or threatened by another child who is usually bigger, stronger, or older than he or she is.

2. *Ask the children:*

> Who can tell me some of the ways children do mean and bullying things to one another?

> What does it feel like to be bullied? What if the person is being bullied every day?

> What should a child do who is being bullied by someone? What should you do if you see another child being bullied?

> Accept some answers from the children for each of the questions.

3. After the discussion, continue with the following demonstration. Say:

> I am going to read a list of some bullying and mean actions that children your age might do. Raise your hand if you ever see that happening in your school or neighborhood. Raise your hand high if you see it often. (Demonstrate) Raise your hand low if you only see it sometimes. (Demonstrate and begin to read the following actions.)

- A child pushes others out the way to be first in line.

- A child tattles on someone just to get them in trouble.

- Children laugh at someone who makes a mistake.

- A group of children gang up on someone and beats them up.

- Children say "you can't play" to someone they don't like.

- Children make fun of what one child is wearing to school.

- One child calls another child mean names like "chicken" or "baby."

- Children mimic or make fun of a child who is different.

- One child purposely trips another child.

- One child won't let another child have a fair turn at a game.

4. Follow up on the demonstration by asking the students to apply the same situations to their own actions. Say:

> Now I am going to ask you a hard question: Do you ever act like a bully? You know that God, your parents, and your teachers want you to treat other children with respect and kindness, but do you ever do or say mean and hurtful things to others? I'm going to read the list of bullying actions again. This time I am asking you to do something hard—to raise your hand to show if you do this kind of bullying action very often (raise hand high) or sometimes (raise hand low). If you never do it, don't raise your hand at all. Everyone close your eyes so you can't see how the other children are answering. (Read the list, saying, "Do you ever push . . .", "Do you tattle . . .", etc.)

5. Wrap up the discussion on bullying with a short prayer. Say:

Let's take a moment to talk to God in our hearts about the meanness and bullying that are present in our lives and in the lives of other children. Close your eyes, fold your hands, and pray with me: Dear God, please forgive me for the times I have been mean to others. Teach me to be kind and respectful to other children, even those who are not kind and respectful to me. Please take special care of the children who always seem to be bullied and picked on. Help the children who act like bullies to learn how to respect others and be kind to them. Help all children to know that you love them too and want them to learn how to love others. Guide us all, parents and children, in helping you to make our world a place where everyone feels safe and loved. Amen.

F. Large Group Review Activity

1. In three different corners of the room, hang three signs that read Physical Abuse, Emotional Abuse, Sexual Abuse. Say:

> I'm going to read a little scenario that shows one of these three kinds of abuse being done by an adult or a child. When I do, I want you to stand under the sign that tells the kind of abuse portrayed in the scenario.

Choose four or five of the scenarios from the list on page 70. Read a statement. Wait for the children to move. Then call the children back to you and read another statement. After four or five moves, ask the children to return to their parents.

2. Give each parent a copy of the "Abuse Scenarios" handout (page 70). Say to the parents:

> Read each of these scenarios with your child and ask her/him to tell you what kind of abuse is portrayed in the scenario. Then discuss with your child what he/she should do if faced with a situation like that.

G. Respect Banner

As the families finish their discussion, give each family the *Respect Banner* handout (page 71), markers, scissors, a sheet of 8 1/2" x 11" construction paper, and a bible. Tell them to follow the instructions for making the banner.

1. *When all the banners are completed, say:*

> The banner is intended to remind your family of the importance of respecting themselves and others. Take it home and hang it on the wall or the refrigerator door.

H. Closing Prayer

Ask the families to stand for a closing prayer. Read together the Prayer of St. Francis that is on the prayer handout sheet and listed below. After the prayer, suggest that the family used the prayer for meals everyday for a week. Challenge the children (and adults!) to memorize it.

Prayer of St. Francis

Lord, make me an instrument of your peace.

Where there is hatred, let me sow love.

Where there is injury, pardon.

Where there is doubt, faith.

Where there is sadness, joy.

O Divine Master, grant that I may not so much seek

To be consoled as to console,

To be understood as to understand;

To be loved as to love;

For it is in giving that we receive,

It is in pardoning that we are pardoned,

And it is in dying that that we are born to eternal life.

Amen.

Thank everyone for coming.

FAMILY INTERVIEW

- Name three things your family likes to do.

1. _____

2. _____

3. _____

- Write the name of each person in your family. Decide one thing that makes each person in your family special and write a word or phrase next to each person's name.

Example: Eric—good at music; Anna—kind.

_____   _____

_____   _____

_____   _____

_____   _____

- Talk about ways you keep your family safe. Write two of the ways below.

Example: Wear seat belts in the car.

1. _____

2. _____

• TYPES OF ABUSE •

IT IS IMPORTANT FOR ALL OF US TO UNDERSTAND
WAYS IN WHICH A CHILD MIGHT NOT BE SAFE.
HERE ARE SOME OF THE WAYS.

• Physical Abuse •

Physical abuse is when someone hurts our bodies in a physical way.

What are some kinds of physical abuse?

Why is it not OK to treat each other in those ways?

• Emotional Abuse •

Our emotions are about how we feel. Emotional abuse is when someone older or bigger does or says something that makes a child feel badly.

What are some ways to hurt a person's feelings?

How might someone feel if they are teased, bullied, or made fun of?

What are some ways a child might hurt another child's feelings?

Bullying is a form of emotional abuse. What are ways a child could be bullied?

Adults can also hurt a child emotionally by ignoring or neglecting a child or not showing love and affection to a child. What are ways an adult might hurt a child in this way?

• Sexual Abuse •

Everyone has private parts of his or her body. They are the parts of our bodies that a bathing suit covers. Only a few certain people have reason to touch those parts of us, like a doctor who is giving a person medical treatment or a parent who is bathing a young child. Sexual abuse is when the private parts of a person's body are not treated with respect. It is when someone feels confused, hurt, or uncomfortable by the way another person touches the private parts of a person's body.

It is never OK for someone to touch another person in a way that makes him or her feel uncomfortable or hurt and confused. Why not?

How would someone feel if another person touched him or her in this way?

What should a child do if someone touches the private parts of their body?

What should you do if you think someone you know is being abused physically, emotionally, or sexually?

Write the names of five people you could tell if you, or someone you know, was hurt in any of these ways.

1. _____

2. _____

3. _____

4. _____

5. _____

There are the Big Three Rules to remember if anyone touches you in any way that makes you feel confused, or uncomfortable, or that hurts you.

    1. Say No.

    2. Get away.

    3. Tell someone you trust.
       (Keep telling until someone listens.)

ABUSE SCENARIOS

1. Some bigger children are teasing a smaller child on the playground. They are calling the person "Weakling," "Big Baby," and "Chicken."

2. You are at a family gathering. You see one of your relatives who you don't know very well. He is pushing his teenage son against a wall in a very rough manner, and it seems as though he is speaking to him in loud and angry voice and calling him names like "stupid" and "idiot."

3. You are on a field trip. In the back of the bus you see an older child squeezing a younger child in the seat against the side of the bus. The older child is laughing. The younger child is crying.

4. You are at the mall. As you walk out of the restroom in an empty hall a man you do not know follows you out and offers you some money for no reason.

5. A coach from your soccer team yells when you miss a goal. He says to you, "Can't you do anything right? Why do you even bother to come to the game if you are going to make so many mistakes?"

6. You are away from home at a camp where you sleep over in a bunkhouse at night. One of the counselors seems to like you more than the other kids and always wants to be alone with you. Sometimes the counselor touches you in ways that make you feel confused and uncomfortable.

7. Your friend has an older brother. He and a group of his friends start teasing you about your appearance and making comments about your body. They are laughing but you don't think it is funny. You want them to stop doing it.

8. You are at your friends' house and their parents aren't home. Your friends want you to watch a movie that is full of sex and violence and that you know your parents would not approve of.

9. The new girl in your class is being laughed at and picked on because the other kids thinks she talks and dresses funny.

10. Your friends are on the Internet passing along gossip and mean messages about someone in your class.

11. The person who sits behind you in class is always poking you, pulling your hair, and kicking your chair. When you turn around, you are the one who gets scolded by the teacher.

12. There is someone in school who is very talkative and popular, but he or she isn't friends with you. You feel like doing something that would make this person look stupid in front of your friends.

RESPECT BANNER

1. CUT OUT THE BANNER SHAPE.

2. WRITE YOUR FAMILY NAME ON THE BANNER.

3. WRITE THE WORD *RESPECT* SOMEWHERE ON YOUR BANNER.

4. CHOOSE ONE OF THE FOLLOWING SCRIPTURE QUOTES TO WRITE ON YOUR BANNER.

   Genesis 1:27
   1 Corinthians 13:13
   1 John 3:18

5. ADD ANY PICTURES OR SYMBOLS.

6. GLUE THE BANNER ON A PIECE OF CONSTRUCTION PAPER.

PRAYER OF ST. FRANCIS

Lord, make me an instrument of your peace.

Where there is hatred, let me sow love.

Where there is injury, pardon.

Where there is doubt, faith.

Where there is sadness, joy.

O Divine Master, grant that I may not so much seek

To be consoled as to console;

To be understood as to understand;

To be loved as to love;

For it is in giving that we receive,

It is in pardoning that we are pardoned,

And it is in dying that that we are born to eternal life.

Amen.

ABUSE

RESPECT

BULLYING

Learning about

L I F E

for Children in Grades 5 and 6 and Their Parents

Session Introduction

This session is designed to help parents discuss with their children in grades 5 and 6 some basic concepts concerning the four kinds of relationships that spell the acronym LIFE (Love, Infatuation, Friendship, and Exploitation). The concept of sexual abuse, as an extreme kind of exploitation, is presented in this context.

In the first activity, family groups work together to name their friends and the people they love, and to show how friendship and love are different from each other. Next they name couples the family knows—married, engaged, or dating—and the parents explain to their children how infatuation (or being in love) is different from love and friendship. The family groups then list the ways that people hurt, abuse, or exploit each other. Finally, they work together as families to list the things every child should learn about each of the four kinds of relationships.

Next the family groups do activities that help the children think about the *feelings* connected with each of the kinds of relationships, and the kinds of *touch* usually associated with each.

The program director then asks the children to come forward and sit on the floor near him or her and invites the parents to sit on chairs behind them. The parents are given a handout containing the content to be presented to the children. The director then teaches the children some of the difficult concepts concerning sexual abuse—what it is, who does it, how it happens, what to do if it should happen to you or a friend. After the teaching, the children go back to the family groups where the parents review the lesson with their children.

The session ends with the writing and reading of feedback statements and a prayer in which the parents bless their children.

Who This Session Is For

Children in grades 5 and 6 with their parents

Goals

- To help children understand four basic kinds of relationships—Love, Infatuation, Friendship, and Exploitation—and the difference between them.

- To help children understand that one of the major aspects of growing up is learning how to give and receive love.

- To help children understand the feelings associated with the various kinds of relationships and the kinds of touch used to express each.

- To help children become aware of the reality of sexual abuse as an extreme form of exploitation.

- To teach children how to respond to any experience of sexual abuse—past, present, or future.

- To begin the healing process for any child who may have been abused in the past.

Materials

- Bible, candle, and holy water for closing prayer

- lap boards

- water-based markers (one set for each family)

- pens or pencils (one set for each family)

- a sheet of twenty multi-colored circular stickers (opaque, not transparent) large enough (3/4") to write on (one sheet for each family)

Preparations:

- Duplicate the LIFE double-sided half-sheets, pages 87–90 (one set for each family). The "What every child needs . . ." goes on the back of each letter.

- Prepare a transparency or print the *Big Three Rules* chart (page 94) on newsprint or a board.

- Duplicate the *Feeling Words* list handout page 91.

- Write your name and number, and the names and numbers of the other adults the child could call, on the *Feedback Sheet*. Duplicate (one copy for each person).

- Duplicate the double-sided *Parent Handout*, pages 92–93 (one for each parent).

- Duplicate *The Big Three* poster or a transparency on heavy cardstock, after putting your name and phone number on the master, page 102 (one for each child).

- Pre-assign seating arrangements, each family in a separate space (e.g., at opposite ends of cafeteria tables). Number the groupings.

- Provide marking pens (water-based) and writing pens or pencils for each group.

- Prepare transparencies teaching charts for the material on pages 95–101. The questions and answers in this section can be printed on 8 1/2" x 11" cardstock.

- Prepare someone to read the scripture passage for the prayer: Mark 12:28–31.

Grades 5 and 6 Lesson Plan

A. Understanding Four Basic Kinds of Personal Relationships: LIFE

Seat the participants at tables, with family groups together. Designate a number for each group.

1. Distribute the "F" half-sheets, one to each family group, and say:

> This activity is going to help you to understand four different kinds of personal relationships. We will start with the most basic relation-ship of all, **Friendship**. Work together as a family group to think of the best friends of each person in your family. Write their names inside the large F on your chart. (Allow time.)

2. Distribute the "L" half-sheets and say:

> Now let's take the letter L, which stands for **Love**. Inside the L each person should write the names of the people who love you and the people you love.

Allow time, then say:

> Now take a few minutes to discuss with your family these two kinds of relationships (friendship and love). How are they the same? How are they different? What has to happen for friendship to become love?

Invite a child from three tables (e.g., group 3, 5, 9) to come forward and explain how their families explained the difference. Then invite three more children to come forward and do the same.

3. Pass out the "I" half-sheets and say:

> Now let's look at the I, which stands for **Infatuation** or being **In love**. (Side note to adults: We are using the word "infatuation" more broadly than its normal use in society. We use the I to stand for the whole spectrum of sexual attraction—all the way from just being interested in someone, to falling in love, to being sexually intimate.) This letter stands for the special kind of relationship a person has with a husband or wife, a "boyfriend" or "girlfriend." Young people usually use the word "like" to stand for this kind of relationship, as in "Jimmy likes Susie." Think of the couples your family knows— married couples, engaged couples, or dating couples. Then draw little hearts inside the I and put the couples' initials inside the hearts.

4. *Allow time, then say:*

> Parents, take some time now to explain to your child how an Infatuation relationship is different from Love and different from Friendship.

Again, call on the children from a few tables to tell what they learned.

5. *Pass out the "E" half-sheet and say:*

> The E on our chart stands for a bad kind of relationship, **Exploitation**. We are going to use this word to stand for any relationship where one person uses, abuses, or hurts another person. This time, instead of writing names in the letter, we will write some of the ways people hurt other people. Let's start with **bullying**. (Tell someone to write that word in the E, and then explain that a person who bullies someone is using that person to make himself/herself feel powerful.) Now work together with your family to think of other ways we *use* other people—to get what we want, to get ahead, to feel good about ourselves at the expense of someone else. Allow time, then have individuals call out some of the words they have written. (Possible answers include: picking on, stealing, teasing, pulling pranks, gossip, making fun, revenge, not sharing, getting even, calling names, tattling.)

B. Growing Up Is Learning about Relationships

1. *Say:*

> One of the most important tasks of growing up is learning about these four kinds of relationships. All children have to learn how to develop good relationships, how to avoid bad ones, how to recognize each kind of relationship when they are experiencing it, and how to deal with the feelings that come with each kind of relationship. Now I'd like you to turn over the Friendship sheet and make a list on the back of some of the important things you are learning, or have already learned, about friendship. (Allow time.)

2. *Continue. Say:*

> Next take the letter L. Write some things every child needs to learn about love. Follow the same process for the I and then for the E.

3. Dialogue with the children.

Have the children from three groups come to the front with the letter F and share the things on their list. Ask questions like: "Have you learned that lesson yet? Who taught you about that?" Follow the same process for each of the other letters.

C. Feelings in Relationships

1. *Give each family group the* Feeling Words *handout and a sheet of multi-colored dots. Say:*

> Let's think about the *feelings* that go with the different kinds of relationships. How do you feel when you are with a good friend? With a grandparent who loves you? With someone you are in love with? With someone who is exploiting or using you? Work together as a family. Start with the F. Think about how you feel when you are with a friend. You can write the names of the feelings on the dots, or draw the face that fits the feeling, then put the dots on the half-sheets for F. Do the same for each letter. Try to think of five different feelings for each kind of relationship. You can use the same feeling for more than one letter.

D. Touch in Relationships

1. *Say:*

> One of the ways we show our feelings is by the way we touch each other. There are different kinds of touch for different kinds of relationships. I'm going to name or show you a kind of touch, and you decide what letter it fits with:
>
> * walking arm in arm (ask two girls to demonstrate)
>
> * kicking, hitting, fighting (ask two boys to pretend)
>
> * high five (demonstrate)
>
> * holding hands (take someone's hand and skip)
>
> * holding hands (take someone's hand romantically)
>
> * warm hug (ask a dad to hug his son)
>
> * hand shake (shake hands with one of the adults)
>
> * fun punch (punch someone gently on the shoulder)

- mean punch (ask the children how they know if a punch is fun or mean)

- a hello or good-bye hug (ask a child to pretend he is your nephew and give him a greeting hug)

- hugging and kissing (ask two of the children to pretend they are in love)

- victory hug (ask four boys to come to the front and pretend they are football players who just won a game)

- wrestling

- tickling

2. *Say:*

We can usually tell what a touch means by *how* the person does it. But sometimes we aren't sure. Sometimes a person might punch you in fun and you get mad and punch back with a mean punch. Wrestling and tickling are two kinds of touch that sometimes get mean and even abusive. Talk with your family about the ways you touch each other. Are there any times when you aren't sure about what some touches mean? (Allow time for discussion.)

3. *Continue:*

One area of touch that you will need to learn about when you get to be teenagers is the touch that fits with the letter I—the kind of touch that shows someone that you like them in the special way we call "being in love." When two people are falling in love, they show their feelings for each other by touches that get closer and closer. "I-touching" goes from holding hands, to simple kisses, to longer kisses, to very close hugging. And then it comes to a big STOP sign. On the other side of the stop sign are touches that are only for married people. After two people are married, they show their love for one another in a very special and holy way—by sexual touches and sexual intercourse. God uses these beautiful acts of love as his way to create children and to make a loving family.

E. Sexual Abuse: A Talk to Children

Rearrange the room so that the children can sit close to you on the floor and the parents can sit behind them in semi-circles of chairs. Give the parents an outline of the talk you will be presenting to the children (see page 92–93). Sit on a chair or on the floor close to the children. Have the transparencies or teaching charts (pages 95–105) ready to show as you ask and answer each question. Speak gently and seriously, making eye contact as you speak.

1. *What is sexual abuse?*

> I want to spend some time with you talking about an especially bad kind of exploitation called **sexual abuse**.
>
> As we explained before, sexual touch is supposed to be the sacred and special way married people show their love for one another and create a loving family, but some people use sex just to get good feelings for themselves. They don't really love the person they are touching. They are using and abusing the person to get something for themselves. When a person uses sexual touch in this unloving way, it's called "sexual abuse."
>
> We are telling you about sexual abuse so that you can be very careful not to let it happen to you, and so you will know what to do if it ever does happen, or if it has already happened.

2. *Why are some adults sexual abusers?*

> Adults who abuse children sexually have a very bad psychological problem called **pedophilia**. A person who has this problem is called a **pedophile**. This big word means that the person has a sexual attraction for children. Something in the person's mind makes them want to do sexual things with children. Some pedophiles are attracted to boys, some to girls, and some to both. Some pedophiles have the problem all the time. Some have it only once in a while, especially when they are drunk, high on drugs, or under very severe stress.

3. *Who might be a sexual abuser?*

> You can't tell by looking at a person whether or not they might be a sexual abuser. They might seem to you to be perfectly normal in every other way. They might act kind, nice, fun, even loving. A person who is a sexual abuser might be a:
>
> - **family member**: mother, father, older brother or sister
> - **relative**: aunt, uncle, grandparent, cousin
> - **adult leader**: teacher, coach, scout leader, priest, nun

- **friend**: teenager, neighbor, friend of parents, another child
- **stranger**: Internet user, neighbor, truck driver

4. *What do sexual abusers do to children?*

If you can't tell by looking at a person who might be a sexual abuser, how can you know who to watch out for? You can tell sexual abusers by what they *do*. These are some of the things sexual abusers might do to a child:

- Try to get the child alone

- Give the child alcohol to drink

- Promise to give the child presents or privileges

- Tell the child that he or she is very special

- Show the child sexual pictures, movies, videos

- Take naked or sexual pictures of the child

- Touch the child in a sexual way

- Ask the child to touch them in a sexual way

- Threaten to hurt the child or someone else if the child tells

- Tell the child that the sexual abuse is really the child's fault

5. *How would a child feel if he or she has been sexually abused? What kind of feelings would a child have if he or she is sexually abused?*

The child would probably feel *confused*. There would be many *bad feelings*: scared, embarrassed, ashamed, and guilty. But there might be some *good feelings*, too. When sexual touch happens in the right place with the right person, it is a pleasant, wonderful feeling. It can make a person feel special, excited, loved. A sexual abuser uses this good thing in a bad way. A child who is sexually abused can have both good and bad feelings, which can be very confusing. Sexual touch is especially confusing for a child if the sexual abuser is someone the child loves and trusts.

6. *What should a child do if someone tries to abuse him or her in this way?*

What should you do if a sexual abuser tries to do any of these things to you? There are three big rules, does anyone know what they are?

(See if the children can tell you the answer, then show them the chart and read each rule.)

- Say No.

- Get away.

- Tell someone you trust. (Keep telling until someone listens.)

Recite The Big Three rules together a few times. Then ask several children to say them. Then point to the last item and explain the seriousness of it. Say:

Never accuse someone if it isn't true.

7. *What should a child do if he or she has been abused before?*

Some children who are abused keep the abuse as an awful secret. They are ashamed and afraid to tell anyone. They don't think anyone will believe them. If you have been abused before, we want you to know these things:

- It is important that you tell someone you trust. Those who love you can't help you unless they know what happened. If you tell someone and they don't believe you, keep telling until you find someone who will listen.

- The bad things that happened were not your fault. The person who abused you should have known better. The abuse was the adult's fault, not yours.

- You are good and loveable. The person who abused you did a bad thing to you, but that person did not *make* you bad.

- Sexual abuse is like a bad wound in your mind and heart. The wound needs to be healed. It won't just go away. Those who love you can help you to get better, but it might take a long time.

- God loves you very much and wants you to be healed of this very bad thing that was done to you.

F. Parent Review of the Lesson

Tell the children to return to their family groups. Ask the parents to review the material that was just taught by asking their children the questions on the outline.

G. Big Three Poster

Give each child a Big Three poster (page 94) to be hung in the child's room.

1. *For the Parents*

Ask the parents to work with the children to write on the poster the names and phone numbers of people the child could call if they ever need to "tell someone you trust" about something that has happened to them.

2. *For the Children*

Ask the children to decorate the poster and take it home to hang in a good spot in their bedrooms.

H. Feedback: Questions and Response

Give each child and adult a feedback sheet, a pen or pencil, and a lapboard and ask them to move to a spot where they can be alone and no one will be able to see what they are writing.

1. *Wait until everyone is settled, then say:*

> I want everyone to fill out this feedback sheet telling me how you felt about this lesson. No one should see what you are writing. You can also write any questions you want me to answer. If you want to talk to me privately, please write your name and phone number on the sheet, and I will call you later to make an appointment. On the bottom of the sheet are some phone numbers you could call if you want to talk to me or to someone else at the parish about a problem of sexual abuse. You may tear that part off if you wish. When you are finished, fold your papers in half. I will walk around and collect them.

If you have time, read aloud some of the feedback sheets. Be careful not to disclose any confidential information that might be found on them. Answer any questions.

Be prepared to respond appropriately to any indications of sexual abuse that may be revealed on the feedback papers. Refer the person(s) through the proper channels for reporting sexual abuse as determined by your diocese.

I. Closing Prayer

Gather all of the families around a table containing a bible, a large candle, and a bowl of holy water. Ask the parents to bring the handout with their prayer, come forward with their children, and to stand around the candle.

2. *Scripture Reading*

Begin with the Sign of the Cross. Ask someone to proclaim Jesus' teaching of the Great Commandment from Mark 12:28–31.

3. *Scripture Reflection. Say:*

> God created human beings for love. As we just heard in the scripture reading, the most important of all the commandments is the commandment to love God and to love one another. Let us be silent for a moment and think about the people we love and the people who love us. (Pause.) Let us ask God to forgive us for the times we have failed to love these people or have loved them badly. (Pause.) Let us ask God to help us to learn to love better, especially to love anyone who has hurt us in the past or anyone that we have hurt. (Pause.) Let us thank God for giving us our families as a place where we can learn to give and receive love. (Pause.)

4. *Continue with a blessing. Say:*

> Now I invite each family to come up to the holy water. I ask the parents to bless your children by tracing a cross on their foreheads and saying the blessing you will find on your parent handout:

> "Name, God made you for love. May you love God with all your heart, with all your soul, with all your mind, and with all your strength. May you learn from your family day by day how to love others and how to love yourself. May you be protected always from all forms of abuse. May God forgive you for any way you may have hurt or abused someone else. May you receive love bountifully and give love generously all the days of your life. Amen."

5. *The Lord's Prayer. Say:*

> Let's close this time of prayer and this evening's lesson by joining hands and praying the prayer that Jesus taught us. Our Father. . . .

Love

Infatuation

Some important things every child needs to learn about INFATUATION:

1. _____

2. _____

3. _____

4. _____

5. _____

Some important things every child needs to learn about LOVING:

1. _____

2. _____

3. _____

4. _____

5. _____

Friendship

Exploitation

Some important things every child needs to learn about
EXPLOITATION:

1. _____

2. _____

3. _____

4. _____

5. _____

Some important things every child needs to learn about
BEING A FRIEND:

1. _____

2. _____

3. _____

4. _____

5. _____

FEEDBACK SHEET

Please circle one: father, mother, boy, girl

1. How did you feel about this lesson? What did you learn that you didn't know before?

2. Will this lesson help you to make decisions for your own life as a parent or as a child? Explain your answer.

3. If you have a question you want me to answer to the whole group, write it here:

4. If you would like to talk to someone about anything you heard tonight, please write your name and phone number below.

....

Or tear here and call one of these numbers:

_____

_____

_____

FEELING WORDS:

accepted
cuddly
curious
caring
ashamed
excited
anxious
comfortable
confident
frightened
hopeful
sad
hurt
joyful
fearful
jumpy
longing
mean

lonely
loved
mischievous
trusting
happy
playful
proud
naughty
safe
rebellious
special
worried
stubborn
nervous
surprised
uncertain
silly

Learning about LIFE:

A Family-Based Program on Relationships and Abuse Prevention

For children in grades 5 and 6 with their parents.

Goals:

- To help children understand four basic kinds of relationships—Love, Infatuation, Friendship, and Exploitation—and the difference between them.

- To help children understand that one of the major aspects of growing up is learning how to give and receive love.

- To help children understand the feelings associated with the various kinds of relationships and the kinds of touch used to express each.

- To help children become aware of the reality of sexual abuse as an extreme form of exploitation.

- To teach children how to respond to any experience of sexual abuse—past, present, or future.

- To begin the healing process for any child who may have been abused in the past.

A. Four basic kinds of human relationship: LIFE.

Love: Love is the most beautiful of human relationships. We know it in God's love for us and in the love parents have for their children: always caring, always ready to forgive, always willing to sacrifice, to put the other person first. Love is characterized by commitment, deep respect, trust, and unconditional acceptance.

Infatuation or being **In love:** We use the word "infatuation" in this program to stand for any relationship which involves sexual attraction and sexual feelings. Infatuation includes any degree of a romantic relationship, from just being interested in a certain girl or guy, all the way to being sexually intimate. Adults use the phrase "being in love" for this relationship. Young people usually use the word "like" as in "Johnny likes Suzy."

Friendship: Friendship is the most basic personal relationship. It names the relationship between any two or more people who trust each other and like to be together. Our friends are usually very much like us, but they don't have to be. A friend can be much older than you or much younger, a different race, have a different body build, be the opposite gender (without being a boyfriend or girlfriend). Some people have many friends. Some prefer to have just a few.

---

6. *What should a child do if someone tries to abuse him or her in this way?*

There are three big rules that every child should know by heart.

SAY NO.

GET AWAY.

TELL SOMEONE YOU TRUST. (Keep telling until someone listens.)

NEVER accuse someone if it isn't true.

7. *What should a child do if he or she has been abused before?*

Sometimes children who are abused keep the abuse as an awful secret. They are ashamed and afraid to tell anyone. They don't think anyone will believe them. A child who has been abused before needs to know these things:

- It is important that you tell someone you trust. Those who love you can't help you unless they know what happened. If you tell someone and they don't believe you, keep telling until you find someone who will listen.

- The bad things that happened were not your fault. The person who abused you should have known better. The abuse was the adult's fault, not yours.

- You are good and loveable. The person who abused you did a bad thing to you, but that person did not make you bad.

- Sexual abuse is like a bad wound in your mind and heart that needs to be healed. The wound won't just go away. Those who love you can help you to get better, but it might take a long time.

- God loves you very much and wants you to be healed of this very bad thing that was done to you.

D. Prayer

"Name, God made you for love. May you love God with all your heart, with all your soul, with all your mind, and with all your strength. May you learn from your family day by day how to love others and how to love yourself. May you be protected always from all forms of abuse. May God forgive you for any way you may have hurt or abused someone else. May you receive love bountifully and give love generously all the days of your life. Amen."

Exploitation: This is a relationship based on selfishness and lack of respect for the other person. We can find some degree of exploitation in almost all of our relationships. We often *use* others—to get our way, to get back at someone, to get things we want and shouldn't have. There are small degrees of exploitation like borrowing paper from someone and never paying him or her back. And there are terrible forms of exploitation, like blackmail and sex abuse.

B. Touch in relationships

One of the ways we show people how we feel about them is by the way we touch them. There are different kinds of touches that are usually associated with each of the four kinds of relationships, e.g., a hug, a handshake, a friendly punch, a kiss.

One area of touch that people your age are often confused about is the touch that starts with the letter I—the kind of touch that shows someone that you like them in the special way we call "being in love." When two people are falling in love, they show their feelings for each other by touches that get closer and closer. "I-touching" goes from holding hands, to simple kisses, to longer kisses, to very close hugging. And then it comes to a big STOP sign. On the other side of the stop sign are touches that are only for married people. After two people are married, they show their love for one another in a very special and holy way—by sexual touches and sexual intercourse. God uses these beautiful acts of love as his way to create children and make a loving family.

C. Sexual Abuse

1. What is sexual abuse?

Sexual abuse is an especially bad kind of exploitation.

Some people use sex just to get good feelings for themselves. They don't really love the person they are touching. They are using the other person just to make themselves feel good or powerful. When a person uses sexual touch in an unloving way, it is called "sexual abuse."

2. Why are some adults sexual abusers?

Some adults have a very bad psychological problem called **pedophilia**. A person who has this problem is called a **pedophile**. This big word means that the person has a sexual attraction for children. He or she wants to do sexual things with children. Some pedophiles are attracted to boys, some to girls, some to both. Some pedophiles have the problem all the time. Some have it only once in a while, especially when they are drunk or high on drugs, or under very severe stress.

3. Who might be a sexual abuser?

You can't tell by looking at a person whether or not he or she might be a sexual abuser. A person might seem to you to be perfectly normal in every other way. They might act kind, nice, fun, even loving. A person who is a sexual abuser might be a

- *family member*: mother, father, or older brother or sister
- *relative*: aunt, uncle, grandparent, or cousin
- *adult leader*: teacher, coach, scout leader, priest, nun
- *friend*: teenager, neighbor, friend of parents, or another child
- *stranger*: Internet user, neighbor, or truck driver

4. What do sexual abusers do to children?

If you can't tell by looking at a person who might be a sexual abuser, how can you know whom to watch out for? You can tell sexual abusers by what they do. These are some of the things sexual abusers might do to a child

- Try to get the child alone
- Give the child alcohol or drugs
- Promise to give the child presents or privileges
- Tell the child that he or she is very special
- Show the child sexual pictures, movies, videos
- Take naked or sexual pictures of the child
- Touch the child in a sexual way
- Ask the child to touch them in a sexual way
- Threaten to hurt the child or someone else if the child tells
- Tell the child that the sexual abuse is really the child's fault

5. How would a child feel if he or she has been sexually abused?

A child who is sexually abused often feels *very confused.*

The child might have many *bad feelings*: frightened, embarrassed, ashamed, guilty. But there might be some *good feelings* too. When sexual touch happens in the right place with the right person, it is a pleasant, wonderful feeling. It can make a person feel special, excited, loved. A sexual abuser uses this good thing in a bad way. A child who is sexually abused can have both good and bad feelings, which can be very confusing. Sexual touch is especially confusing for a child if the sexual abuser is someone the child loves and trusts.

THE BIG THREE

WHAT TO DO IN CASE OF SEXUAL ABUSE

- **SAY NO.**

- **GET AWAY.**

- **TELL SOMEONE YOU TRUST.**

  (Keep telling until someone listens.)

People I can trust

Name

Phone

_____   _____

_____   _____

_____   _____

_____   _____

_____   _____

_____   _____

What is sexual abuse?

pedophilia

pedophile

Who might be a sexual abuser?

Learning about
LIFE

family member: mother, father, older brother or sister

relative: aunt, uncle, grandparent, cousin

adult leader: teacher, coach, scout leader, priest, nun

friend: teenager, friend of parents, neighbor, babysitter, another child

stranger: Internet user, truck driver, bus driver, shopper

What do sexual abusers do to children?

- get you alone
- give alcohol or drugs
- make promises or give presents
- show sexual pictures or videos
- take sexual photos of you
- tell you that you are special

- touch you sexually
- make you touch them sexually
- tell you not to tell
- threaten to hurt you (or someone else) if you tell
- try to do it again

Bad Feelings:

- scared
- embarrassed
- ashamed
- guilty
- hurt
- dirty

Good Feelings

- special
- excited
- loved
- grown up
- accepted
- confused

THE BIG THREE

WHAT TO DO IN CASE OF SEXUAL ABUSE

SAY NO.

GET AWAY.

TELL SOMEONE YOU TRUST.

(Keep telling until someone listens.)

NEVER accuse someone if it isn't true.

Learning about
LIFE

What does a person who has been (or is being) sexually abused need to know?

- Talk to someone you trust. Keep talking until you find someone who can help you.

- The abuse is not your fault. It is the abuser's fault.

- You are good. The abuse is bad.

- Sexual abuse is like a serious wound that needs to be healed. It won't just go away.

- God loves you and wants you to be healed.

Learning about

L I F E

for Children in Grades 7 and 8 and Their Parents

Session Introduction

This session is designed to help the parents of children in grades 7 and 8 review with their children some basic concepts concerning the four kinds of relationships that spell the acronym LIFE (Love, Infatuation, Friendship, and Exploitation). The concept of sexual abuse, as a form of exploitation, is presented in this context.

In the opening activity, small groups of adolescents with their parents examine current movies, books, TV shows, and videos to see how the four kinds of relationships are presented in them. The young people are then invited to gather toward the front of the room with the parents behind them. The director talks to them about the various signs of affection that are used to communicate the deepening of a sexual relationship—from talking, to holding hands, to hugging and kissing, and so on. It is emphasized that sexual touch and sexual intercourse are always to be saved for the committed love relationship of marriage.

A presentation on sexual abuse follows. Mention is made of the fact that sometimes young adolescents can get involved with sexual activities for many different reasons: out of curiosity, in response to peer pressure, or just for excitement. The director challenges them to make serious personal decisions about their growing sexual development, and to pray every day for the graces they will need, as they move into their high school years, to respect the beautiful gift of sexuality in themselves and in others.

The session closes with the parents blessing their children using the a prayer called *Choose Life* from the book of Deuteronomy.

Who This Session Is For

Children in grades 7 and 8 with their parents

Goals

- To help young adolescents understand four basic kinds of relationships—Love, Infatuation, Friendship, and Exploitation—and the difference between them.

- To help young adolescents understand that one of the major aspects of growing up is learning how to give and receive love.

- To help young adolescents understand the feelings associated with the various kinds of relationships and the kinds of touch used to express each.

- To help young adolescents become aware of the reality of sexual abuse as a major form of exploitation.

- To help young adolescents realize that some sexually-related activities that they or their peers are involved in may be exploitative and abusive.

- To teach young adolescents how to respond to any experience of sexual abuse—past, present, or future.

- To begin the healing process for any adolescent who may have been abused in the past.

Materials

- slips of blank paper, approximately 2" x 2" (about five slips for each person)

- chalkboard or whiteboard

- pens or pencils (one for each person)

- lap boards (one for each person)

Preparations:

- Duplicate the *LIFE* handout, page 118, (one for each person).

- Duplicate the double-sided *Parent Handout*, pages 119–120, (one for each parent).

- Put names and phone numbers on the *Feedback Sheet*. Duplicate the *Feedback Sheet/Choose Life Prayer*, page 121 (one for each person).

- Prepare transparencies or teaching charts for the material on pages 122–135. The questions and answers can be printed on 8 1/2" x 11" cardstock (see pages 122–135).

Grades 7 and 8 Lesson Plan

A. Understanding Four Basic Kinds of Relationships: LIFE

Create small groups of two or three teens with their parents. Give each group a stack of 2" x 2" slips of paper (about five for each person).

1. *Say:*

> Work together as a group to think of the titles of movies, TV shows, songs, and books in which *relationships* are an important theme. Write one title on each of these little pieces of paper. (Allow time.)

2. *Pass out copies of the LIFE. handout. Then, say:*

> Put your pile of titles aside for a few moments. I want to tell you about four basic kinds of personal relationships which spell the acronym LIFE. You might remember learning about these in earlier sessions of this program.
>
> Let's begin with the F—**Friendship**—the relationship you all know the most about. Friendship is the most basic personal relationship. It names the connection between any two or more people who trust each other and like to be together. Our friends are usually very much like us, but they don't have to be. Raise your hand if you have a friend who is much older than you (pause), much younger (pause), a different race (pause), of a different body build (pause), of the opposite gender (but not a boyfriend or girlfriend). Some people have many friends. Some prefer to have just a few.
>
> On your handout, you will find several key words written around the F. I would ask the *teens* in your group to take turns, pick a word from the chart, and explain what that word says about friendship. You might also think of other words or phrases you think should be added to the chart.

3. *Allow time. Then ask if there are words any group added to the friendship box. After hearing some of those words, say:*

> Next we are going to talk about *love*. For now we are going to focus on love as distinct from romance. Love is the most beautiful of human relationships. Think about God's love for us and the love parents have for their children: always there, always caring, always ready to forgive, always willing to sacrifice, to put the other person first.

Commitment, unconditional acceptance, deep respect, and trust characterize love.

This time I would like the *parents* to do the talking. Take turns, choose a word from the L box, and explain what it says about love as you have experienced it. There may also be other words your group wants to add to the L box.

4. *Ask if there are any words to add to the Love box, then say:*

Now let's look at the I box—**Infatuation**. In this program we use the word "infatuation"—or the I-Factor—to stand for any relationship which involves sexual attraction and sexual feelings. Infatuation includes any degree of a romantic relationship, from just being interested in a certain girl or guy, all the way to being sexually intimate. Adults usually use the phrase "being in love" for this relationship. Young teens use the word "like" as in "Johnny likes Suzy." Notice the various I words written inside infatuation in the I box.

This time, parents and teens will each take a turn, starting with the youngest person in the group and going around the circle. Choose a word and explain why you think that word is in this box. Add other words that seem to fit.

5. *Check on words to add, then say:*

Finally we are going to look at the E—**Exploitation**. This is a negative relationship—one based on selfishness and lack of respect for the other person. There are small degrees of exploitation, like always borrowing paper from someone and never paying him or her back. And there are terrible forms of exploitation, like blackmail and sexual abuse. If we were honest with ourselves, we would probably find some degree of exploitation in almost all of our relationships. We often *use* others—to get our way, to get back at someone, to get things we want and shouldn't have.

This time, start with the oldest person in the group. Again take turns picking a word and explaining what it has to say about exploitative relationships. Allow time, then ask if there are any words to add.

6. *Write the four letters on the board, each a different size. Say:*

Most relationships are a combination of two or three of these letters. (Aside to the parents: A marriage is usually a combination of all four. To do an interesting analysis of your marriage, you could divide it into five-year periods and see how much L, I, F, and E could be found in each period. We won't ask you to do that in front of the kids, though!) On your handout, you will see a row of combinations: FE, IF, IE, LI, LE, LF. Take turns in your group describing what each of these relationships would be like.

7. *Write on the board a large F and small e, and a small f and large E.*

Also show the contrast between a relationship that is mostly **F** with a little bit of **e** and one that is just a small **f** and a lot of **E**, etc. Now put one LIFE handout in the center of your table and go back to your pile of titles. Decide together whether each song, show, or book is mostly about Love, mostly about Infatuation, mostly about Friendship, or mostly about Exploitation. When you have decided, put the title in the square on your sheet. Some titles will fit on the line between two or more squares.

8. *Allow time, then assign each group one letter.*

Ask them to pick one title that is a good example of that kind of relationship and to send one teen to the front of the room to explain their pick.

B. Touch: Love or Exploitation

Invite the young people to bring their chairs and move up close to you and to the board. Then invite the adults to move in behind them. Give the parents an outline of the material you will be presenting in this next session.

1. *Begin a discussion with the young people. Say:*

One of the ways that an infatuation relationship is different from a friendship relationship is the way we show the other person that we care about them. Who can tell me some of the ways you let your friends know that you like them? (Responses will include calling them, sitting with them, going places together, playing games together, sleeping over, etc.) Are there any physical signs of affection that you might use with your friends (e.g., friendly punches, an arm around shoulders, victory hugs)?

2. *Continue. Say:*

Touch plays a much bigger role in an infatuation relationship than it does in a friendship relationship. Does anyone have an older brother or sister who has a boyfriend or girlfriend? What kinds of touching do you see them sharing (e.g., holding hands, hugging, kissing)?

3. *Write on the board: **T >> HH >> H+K >> PK >> ST >> SI**. See if anyone can tell you what this set of letters might mean, then say:*

> The touching in an infatuation relationship follows a certain pattern of development. (Point to the letters on the board as you explain them.) It moves from just **talking** to someone, to **holding hands**, to **hugging and kissing**, to **passionate kissing**, to **sexual touching**, to **sexual intercourse**. There are some important things you need to know about the progression along that line.
>
> - God planned the whole line. It is part of God's plan for creating loving families where children are born and cared for.
>
> - Each step along the line is meant by God to be a sign of a deepening love relationship. (Draw an opening wedge above the line to symbolize love growing.) As you learn to love a person more and more, your way of showing that love gets more and more intimate.
>
> - The last two steps on the line, sexual touch and sexual intercourse, are meant *only* for those who love each other so much that they want to spend their whole life together, creating a family and having children. They make a public promise that they will love one another until death. What is that promise called? (Put a box around **ST** and **SI** and write the word **marriage** above the box.)

4. *Conclude this presentation. Say:*

> In God's plan, sexual touch is meant to be a sign of deep **LOVE**. (Write the word in capital letters on the board.) But it can also become a very serious kind of **EXPLOITATION**. (Write the word under Love on the board.) Another name for this kind of exploitation is **SEXUAL ABUSE**. (Write next to exploitation.)

C. Sexual Exploitation, Sexual Abuse, Harassment

Present the next session using transparency or charts containing the questions and answers given below (see page 122–135). Show the group a chart with the question, then show the charts with the answers as you explain each one. Give examples and details as fitting.

1. *Why should we teach adolescents about sexual abuse?*

- So that they will know how to avoid being abused sexually by anyone.

- So that they will know what to do if they have been or are being sexually abused.

- So that they will know how to help a friend who has been or is being sexually abused.

- So that they will never *be* people who abuse others sexually.

- So that they will never falsely accuse someone of sexual abuse.

2. *What is pedophilia?*

Pedophilia is a serious psychological problem that causes an adult to be sexually attracted to children and to look for opportunities to do sexual things with them. Adults who abuse children sexually are called pedophiles. Some pedophiles are attracted to boys, some to girls, and some to both. Some have the problem all the time, some only when they are drunk or high or when they are under very great stress.

3. *Who might be a sexual abuser?*

Children are taught at a young age to be aware of strangers who might do bad things to them. But a sexual abuser is more often not a stranger but someone a child or teen knows and trusts. A sexual abuser might be a:

- **family member**: mother, father, older brother or sister

- **relative**: aunt, uncle, grandparent, cousin

- **adult leader**: teacher, coach, scout leader, priest, nun

- **friend**: teenager, neighbor, friend of parents, another child

- **stranger**: Internet user, neighbor, truck driver

4. *How does a pedophile operate? How do young people get pulled into his or her web?*

A pedophile is usually a very slick operator. A pedophile is always on the lookout for young people who are vulnerable and who can be used by the pedophile for sexual pleasure. These are some of the things sexual abusers might do to a child or young teenager:

- Try to get the child/teen alone

- Give the child/teen alcohol or other drugs

- Promise to give them presents or privileges

- Build their trust, also their parents' trust

- Play on their natural curiosity about sex

- Show them sexual pictures, movies, videos

- Take naked or sexual pictures of them

- Touch the child/teen in a sexual way

- Ask the child/teen to touch them in a sexual way

- Force the child/teen to do sexual things (oral sex, intercourse)

- Swear the child/teen to secrecy

- Threaten to hurt the child/teen or someone else if he/she tells

- Tell the child/teen that the sexual abuse is really his/her fault

5. *How would a person feel who had been sexually abused?*

The response of children or adolescents to sexual abuse is often *confusion*. They have many negative feelings like shame, embarrassment, guilt, hurt, and betrayal. But they might also have some good feelings. Sexual touch is supposed to be a pleasant experience. The abuser may be gentle and seem to be loving. The victim might believe what the abuser has said to them, and feel special and loved. Sometimes the victim doesn't realize until much later that they have been lied to and used.

6. *Are young teens ever guilty of sexual abuse?*

Sometimes young people your age or older do sexual things out of *curiosity*, in response to *peer pressure*, to *act grown up*, to *feel powerful*, or just for the *excitement*. I am going to read a list of activities that some teens your age do, things that could be considered sexual exploitation, abuse, or harassment. Raise your hand if you know about kids who have done the thing. Raise your hand high if you know it happens a lot, low if you just heard about it once or twice.

- making fun of the sexual areas of someone's body

- touching, grabbing, or groping the sexual areas

- bullying someone in a sexual way

- pressuring someone into doing sexual things (Saying: "You would if you loved me.")

- playing sex games at parties

- looking at porn on the Internet

- gossiping about someone's sexual activity

- bragging about their own sexual activity with someone

- making fun of someone's sexual experience or lack of it

- leading a person along just to see how far they will go

- sexual kissing (open-mouthed kissing)

- oral sex

- sexual intercourse

Turn to the parents and ask:

How do you feel about the kids' response to that list? What can you as parents do about it?

Turn back to the teens and say:

As an adolescent, you need to make some serious personal decisions about your own growing sexuality. God and your parents want you to become strong, independent young men and women who can give and receive love honestly and truly. They want you to choose to avoid any activity that is exploitative, or that shows disrespect for yourself or someone else. Your parents can teach you and protect you only so far, then it is up to you. Pray every day—for yourself and for your friends—that you will always respect the beautiful gift of sex and use it only according to God's plan.

7. *What does a person who has been (or is being) sexually abused need to know?*

Sexual abuse can cause serious traumatic problems in the life of a person who has been abused. Anyone who has been—or is being—abused, needs to remember these things:

- God loves you very much and wants you to be healed of the bad effects of this traumatic experience in your life.

- You are a good and lovable person. The person who abused you did a bad thing to you, but that did not make you a bad person.

- It is important that you talk to an adult whom you trust about the abuse. Those who love you can't help you unless they know what happened. If you tell someone and that person doesn't believe you, keep telling until you find someone who will listen.

- The sexual abuse is not your fault. An abuser will try to blame you for what happened, but the abuse is the adult's fault, not yours.

- Sexual abuse is like a serious wound that needs to be healed. The healing might take a long time and much counseling and guidance. Those who love you can help you to get better, but you must let them help.

- If a friend tells you that they are being abused, you *must* find an adult who can help the friend. This is a problem that is much too big for an adolescent to try to solve.

D. Feedback

Pass out the Feedback Sheets (page 121), lap boards, and pens.

1. *Explain the following evaluation activity. Say:*

> Please move to a spot in the room where you can be alone and no one can see what you are writing. You will need a lap board, a pen, and a Feedback Sheet handout.

> What you write on the feedback sheet will be completely confidential. You may sign your name or leave it anonymous. When you finish writing, fold the paper in half and I will come around to collect them.

2. *Collect the feedback sheets.*

> If you have time, read some of them aloud to the group. Be careful not to read anything that might be of a sensitive or personal nature.

Follow up on any indications given in the feedback sheets that someone needs further help and counseling. Direct the person(s) through the proper channels for reporting sexual abuse in your diocese.

E. Closing Prayer

Distribute copies of the *Choose Life* handout (page 121) to each person.

1. *Say:*

> Everybody stand in family groups. We are going to close our session this evening with an ancient blessing found in the book of Deuteronomy. Parents, please place your right hand on your child's shoulder and pray this blessing with me. Let us include in our blessing not only these children who are here tonight, but all of their friends and classmates who are not here, and all young people who are growing up sexually in this difficult time.

Pray the *Choose Life* prayer together, then close with a sign of peace.

LIFE

There are four basic kinds of human relationships:

Love: Love is the most beautiful, the most rewarding, and the most challenging of all relationships. Love involves mutual acceptance, respect, and trust. Love shows itself in commitment and a willingness to sacrifice for the one loved. Love is enduring, patient, forgiving, and encouraging. Love lasts through thick and thin. Learning to give and to receive love is the most important task any human being faces.

Infatuation (or being "in love"): Romantic infatuation is a relationship involving deep emotion and sexual attraction. Infatuation is exciting and all-absorbing. It is characterized by extremes of happiness and dejection, by exclusiveness and jealousy. Infatuation seeks expression in kisses, hugs, touches, and sometimes sexual intercourse. Infatuation is often called "love," but it isn't the same as love. Unless it is accompanied by real love, infatuation won't last.

Friendship: Friendship is comfortable and easy, enriching and fun. It is based on mutual trust, understanding, acceptance, and enjoyment. Friendship is not exclusive or possessive but leaves the other free. A person can have many friends at once, friends of both sexes, friends of all ages, races, and religions. Some friendships last a lifetime. The best of them grow into love.

Exploitation: Exploitation is a relationship based on selfishness. We exploit others when we use them to get what we want and don't really care how they think or feel. Exploitative relationships lack respect, concern, and commitment; they are deceptive and self-serving. Manipulation, ridicule, abuse, blackmail, pranks, vandalism, and casual sex are all forms of exploitation. If we are honest, we can discover some degree of exploitation in most of our relationships.

Most relationships are a mixture of two or more of the above elements. Describe a relationship that includes the combinations listed below:

FE   IF   IE   LI   LE   LF

Infatuation
joy, exclusiveness, excitement, in love, interested, kissing, ecstasy, jealousy, hurt, touch, fickleness, depression, day dreams, love letters, intercourse, intimacy, loss of appetite, total involvement

Exploitation
arrogance, abuse, blackmail, pranks, take advantage, take for granted, insensitive, convenience, use, manipulation, curiosity, mocking, experimentation

Love
caring, sensitivity, trust, willing to help, deep mutual respect, forgiveness, consideration, unconditional acceptance, permanence, commitment, self-sacrifice, kindness, understanding

Friendship
ease, dependability, acceptance, approval, companionship, belonging, laughter, trust, openness, challenge, fun, freedom, understanding

PARENT HANDOUT

Learning about LIFE:

A Family-Based Program on Relationships and Abuse Prevention

For children in grades 7 and 8 with their parents.

Goals:

- To help adolescents understand four basic kinds of relationships—Love, Infatuation, Friendship, and Exploitation—and the difference between them.

- To help adolescents understand that one of the major aspects of becoming an adult is learning how to give and receive love.

- To help adolescents understand, and deal appropriately with, sexual attraction and relationships that have a sexual component.

- To help adolescents understand the feelings associated with the various kinds of relationships and the kinds of touch used to express each.

- To help adolescents become aware of the reality of sexual abuse as a major form of exploitation.

- To help adolescents realize that some sexually-related activities that they or their peers are involved in can be exploitative and abusive.

- To teach adolescents how to respond to any experience of sexual abuse—past, present, or future.

- To begin the healing process for any adolescent who may have been abused in the past.

Four basic kinds of human relationship: LIFE.

Love: Love is the most beautiful, the most rewarding, and the most challenging of all relationships. Love involves mutual acceptance, respect, and trust. Love shows itself in commitment and a willingness to sacrifice for the one loved. Love is enduring, patient, forgiving, and encouraging. Love lasts through thick and thin. Learning to give and to receive love is the most important task any human being faces.

Infatuation: We use the word "infatuation" in this program to stand for any relationship which involves sexual attraction and sexual feelings. Infatuation includes any degree of a romantic relationship, from just being interested in a certain girl or guy, all the way to being sexually intimate. Adults use the phrase "being in love" for this relationship. Young people usually use the word "like" as in "Johnny likes Suzy."

How would a person feel who has been sexually abused?

The response of children and adolescents to sexual abuse is often CONFUSION. They may have many negative feelings like shame, embarrassment, guilt, hurt, and betrayal. But they may also have some good feelings. Sexual touch is supposed to be a pleasant experience. The abuser may be gentle and seem to be loving. The victims might believe what the abuser has said to them, and feel special and loved. Sometimes the victims don't realize until much later that they have been lied to and used.

What does a person who has been (or is being) sexually abused need to know?

Sexual abuse can cause serious traumatic problems in the life of a person who has been abused. Anyone who has been—or is being—abused needs to remember these things:

- God loves you very much and wants you to be healed of the bad effects of this traumatic experience in your life.

- You are a good and lovable person. The person who abused you did a bad thing to you, but that did not make you a bad person.

- It is important that you tell an adult whom you trust. Those who love you can't help you unless they know what happened. If you tell someone and that person doesn't believe you, keep telling until you find someone who will listen.

- The sexual abuse is not your fault. An abuser will try to blame you for what happened, but the abuse is the adult's fault, not yours.

- Sexual abuse is like a serious wound that needs to be healed. The healing might take a long time and much counseling and guidance. Those who love you can help you to get better, but you must let them help.

- If a friend tells you that they are being abused, you *must* find an adult who can help the friend. This is a problem that is much too big for an adolescent to try to solve.

God is love,

and all who live in love

live in God

and God in them.

Friendship: Friendship is the most basic personal relationship. It names the relationship between any two or more people who trust each other and like to be together. Our friends are usually very much like us, but they don't have to be. A friend can be much older than you or much younger, a different race, have a different body build, be the opposite gender (without being a boyfriend or girlfriend). Some people have many friends. Some prefer to have just a few.

Exploitation: This is a relationship based on selfishness and lack of respect for the other person. We can find some degree of exploitation in almost all of our relationships. We often use others—to get our way, to get back at someone, to get things we want and shouldn't have. There are small degrees of exploitation, like always borrowing paper from someone and never paying him or her back. And there are terrible forms of exploitation, like blackmail and sex abuse.

Touch – Love or Exploitation

The touching in an infatuation relationship follows a certain pattern of development. It moves from just **talking** to someone, to **holding hands**, to **hugging and kissing**, to **passionate kissing**, to **sexual touching**, to **sexual intercourse**. Important things you need to know about the progression along that line include.

- God planned the whole line. It is part of God's plan for creating loving families where children are born and cared for.

- Each step along the line is meant by God to be a sign of a deepening love relationship. As you learn to love a person more and more, your way of showing that love gets more and more intimate.

- The last two steps on the line, sexual touch and sexual intercourse, are meant *only* for those who love each other so much that they want to spend their whole life together, creating a family and having children. They make a public promise—marriage—that they will love one another until death.

In God's plan, sexual touch is meant to be a sign of deep LOVE. But it can also become a very serious kind of EXPLOITATION. Another name for this kind of exploitation is SEXUAL ABUSE.

2

Reasons for teaching adolescents about sexual abuse:

- So that they will know how to avoid being abused sexually by anyone.
- So that they will know what to do if they have been or are being sexually abused.
- So that they will know how to help a friend who has been or is being sexually abused.
- So that they will never be people who abuse others sexually.
- So that they will never falsely accuse someone of sexual abuse.

Pedophilia

Adults who abuse children sexually are called *pedophiles*. Pedophilia is a serious psychological problem which causes an adult to be sexually attracted to children and to look for opportunities to do sexual things with them. Some pedophiles are attracted to boys, some to girls, and some to both. Some have the problem all the time, some only when they are drunk, high, or under very great stress.

A person who is a sexual abuser might be a

- *family member:* mother, father, or older brother or sister
- *relative:* aunt, uncle, grandparent, or cousin
- *adult leader:* teacher, coach, scout leader, priest, or nun
- *friend:* teenager, neighbor, friend of parents, or another child
- *stranger:* Internet user, neighbor, or truck driver

How does a pedophile operate?

A pedophile is usually a very slick operator. A pedophile is on the lookout for young people to use for sexual pleasure. Some steps a pedophile uses are:

- gets the child / teen alone
- gives the child / teen alcohol or drugs
- shows them sexual pictures, movies, videos
- convinces them that it is okay to do what he / she says
- uses them sexually: sexual touch, oral sex, intercourse
- promises presents and privileges
- builds their trust, also their parents' trust
- plays on their natural curiosity about sex
- blames them for what happened
- swears them to secrecy
- threatens to hurt them or someone else if they tell

3

Love Yahweh your God
cling to him
and obey his voice

for he has blessed you
and made you his own
let not your heart stray

refuse not to listen
be not drawn away

see, before you is set
blessings and life

disaster and death

choose

the decision is yours

CHOOSE LIFE

so that you
and your children

may live

live in the love
of Yahweh your God.

–adapted from Deuteronomy 30:16–20

Feedback Sheet

Please circle one: father   mother   boy   girl

1. How did you feel about this lesson? What did you learn that you didn't know before?

2. Will this lesson help you to make decisions for your own life as a parent or as a teen? Explain your answer.

3. If you have any questions you want me to answer for the entire group, please write them here.

4. If you would like to talk to someone about anything you heard tonight, please write your name and phone number below.

_____

Or tear here and call one of these numbers

_____

_____

Why teach you about sexual exploitation and sexual abuse?

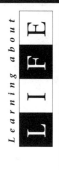

- so you will know how how to avoid being abused

- so you will know what to do if you are (or have been) abused

- so you can help a friend who is being (or has been) abused

- so you will never be a sexual abuser

- so you will never falsely accuse someone of sexual abuse

An adult who uses a child or teen for sexual pleasure is called a **PEDOPHILE.** This serious disorder is called **PEDOPHILIA.**

A pedophile may be a:

family member: father, mother, brother, or sister

relative: aunt, uncle, grandparent, or cousin

adult leader: teacher, coach, scout leader, priest or nun

friend: teenager, friend of parents, neighbor, or babysitter

stranger: Internet user, truck driver, bus driver, or shopper

How does a pedophile operate?

How do young people get pulled into his/her web?

Learning about
LIFE

- gets them alone
- gives them alcohol or drugs
- gives them presents
- makes promises
- builds trust
- plays on their natural curiosity about sex
- shows sexual movies, videos, or pictures

- takes sexual pictures
- touches them in a sexual way
- forces them to do sexual things
- swears them to secrecy
- threatens to hurt them or someone else if they tell
- blames them for what happened

How would a person feel who has been abused sexually?

CONFUSED

Good Feelings:

- special
- excited
- loved
- grown up
- accepted

Bad Feelings:

- scared
- embarrassed
- ashamed
- guilty
- hurt
- dirty
- used

YOUTH sometimes do sexual acts because they

- are curious

- feel peer pressure

- want to act grown up

- want to feel powerful

- want to feel excitement

What does a person who has been (or is being) sexually abused need to know?

- God loves you.

- You are good. The abuse is bad.

- Sexual abuse is not your fault.

- Sexual abuse is like a serious wound that needs to be healed.

- The wound won't go away. It will fester if you don't deal with it.

- Talk to someone you trust. Keep talking until you find someone who can help you heal.

If a friend tells you he/she has been abused, help the person find an adult who can help.

Learning about

L I F E

for Adolescents in Grades 9 and 10

and Their Parents

Session Introduction

This session is designed to help adolescents in grades 9 and 10 and their parents to review (or to learn) some basic concepts concerning the four kinds of relationships that spell the acronym LIFE (Love, Infatuation, Friendship, and Exploitation). The concept of sexual abuse, as a form of exploitation, is presented in this context.

In the opening activity, small groups of adolescents with their parents share some "pearls of wisdom" that life has taught them about LIFE They then look at the difference between relationships with persons of the other gender that are simply friendship, and relationships that include infatuation and sexual attraction.

The young people are then invited to gather toward the front of the room with the parents sitting behind them. The presenter compares for them the relatively rapid movement of an infatuation relationship, with the slow but steady growth of a relationship from friendship to real love. Emphasis is placed on the plan of God that requires us to save intimate sexual touch and sexual intercourse for the committed love relationship of marriage.

A presentation on sexual abuse follows, focusing on the kinds of abusive and exploitative activities that teens their own age sometimes get involved in. The young people then examine the factors that need to be part of their lives for them to make positive, life-giving decisions about their sexuality and to experience healthy romantic relationships.

They then spend quiet time using the *LIFE Report Card* as an examination of conscience to see how they are doing in the process of learning to become loving persons.

The session ends with the writing and reading of feedback statements. The closing prayer is based on the famous passage from 1 Corinthians 13 delineating the qualities of love.

Who this Session Is For

Adolescents in grades 9 and 10 with their parents.

Goals

- To help adolescents understand four basic kinds of relationships—Love, Infatuation, Friendship, and Exploitation—and the difference between them.

- To help adolescents understand that one of the major aspects of becoming an adult is learning how to give and receive love.

- To help adolescents understand, and deal appropriately with, sexual attraction and relationships that have a sexual component.

- To help adolescents understand the feelings associated with the various kinds of relationships and the kinds of touch used to express each.

- To help adolescents become aware of the reality of sexual abuse as a serious form of exploitation.

- To help adolescents realize that sexual activity by and with other adolescents can be exploitative.

- To teach adolescents how to respond to any experience of sexual abuse—past, present, or future.

Materials

- 3″ x 5″ index cards (at least four for each person)

- pens and lap boards (one for each person)

Preparations

- Duplicate on card stock the *Fran/Fred Ike/Ida* handout, page 148, and cut apart (one separate card for each small group).

- Duplicate the *Teen World Realities* and *1 Corinthians Prayer* handouts, page 149 (one for each person). Cut apart.

- Duplicate the double-sided *Parent Handout*, pages 150–151, (one for each parent).

- Duplicate the double-sided *Your LIFE Report Card* handout, pages 152–153, (one for each parent).

- Duplicate the *Feedback Sheet* handout, page 154, after writing all the appropriate names and phone numbers. Cut apart (one separate sheet for each participant).

- Prepare transparencies or teaching charts for the material on pages 155–156. *Optional*: Print the material on page 155–156 (**If it isn't real love—DON'T. If it is real love—WAIT**) onto a poster.

Grades 9 and 10 Lesson Plan

A. Pearls of Wisdom: LIFE

Create small groups of two or three teens with their parents.

1. *Review (or teach) the difference between the four kinds of relationships that have been presented in earlier levels of this program. Say some or all of the following:*

> **Love**: Love is the most beautiful of human relationships. We know it in God's love for us and in the love parents have for their children: always there, always caring, always ready to forgive, always willing to sacrifice, to put the other person first. Love is characterized by commitment, deep respect, trust, and unconditional acceptance.

> **Infatuation**: In this program, we use the word "infatuation"—or the "I-Factor"—to stand for any relationship which involves sexual attraction and sexual feelings. Infatuation includes any degree of a romantic relationship, from just being interested in a certain girl or guy, all the way to being sexually intimate. Adults usually use the phrase "being in love" for this relationship. Young teens use the word "like" as in "Johnny likes Suzy."

> **Friendship**: Friendship is the relationship you all know the most about. Friendship is the most basic personal relationship. It names the connection between any two or more people who trust each other and like to be together. Our friends are usually very much like us, but they don't have to be. Raise your hand if you have a friend who is much older than you (pause), much younger (pause), of a different race (pause), of a different body build (pause), of the opposite gender (but not a boyfriend or girlfriend). Some people have many friends. Some prefer to have just a few.

> **Exploitation**: This is a negative relationship—one based on selfishness and lack of respect for the other person. There are small degrees of exploitation, like always borrowing paper from someone and never paying him or her back. And there are terrible forms of exploitation, like blackmail and sexual abuse. If we were honest with ourselves, we would probably find some degree of exploitation in almost all of our relationships. We often *use* others—to get our way, to get back at someone, to get things we want and shouldn't have.

2. *Give each group a stack of 3" x 5" cards, at least four per participant, and say:*

> The best place to learn about LIFE is *life*. Life has already taught each of you, adults and teens, many important lessons about Love, about Infatuation, about Friendship, and about Exploitation. I want you to think about some of those lessons now and write them on these cards. You will write one card for each of the four kinds of relationships. You may write more if you have time. Write "I've learned that . . ." and the lesson life has taught you about love, or friendship, or infatuation, or exploitation. Put your cards face down in the center of the table as you write them.

3. *Allow time for each person to write at least four cards, then say:*

> Now take turns around the table. Draw a card and read the "pearl of wisdom" found there. Then your group will try to guess whose pearl you just read.

> Allow time, then ask each group to select one pearl and choose a teen to go to the front to read it to everyone.

B. Friendship and Infatuation

Give each group a *Fran/Fred Ida/Ike* card from page 148.

1. *Explain:*

> You have been learning about friendship since you were very young children—how to make friends, how to be a friend, how to deal with friends when they have problems, how to act with people who aren't yet your friends. Developing friendships continues to be an important part of your teen years, but added to it now is the task of dealing with a person who attracts you sexually.

> Your bodies have matured physically and sexually over the past few years, and you have begun to experience some of the feelings that are connected with sexuality. One of the primary life tasks of adolescence is to learn how to deal comfortably with the feelings associated with sexual attraction—that mysterious and exciting reality that this program calls Infatuation or the "I-Factor." In your teen years, you will gradually learn how to be comfortable, respectful, and self-assured in dealing with members of the opposite sex, especially those whom you find sexually attractive.

On your table is a card that says Fran/Fred, Ida/Ike. In this activity, we are going to contrast how one might feel about a person of the other gender who is just a *friend* with how one feels about a person for whom you have the feelings associated with *infatuation*, someone you "like" in the special sense of being a boyfriend or girlfriend. We'll call the friend person Fran or Fred. And we'll call the boyfriend/girlfriend person Ida or Ike. In doing this activity, I want the adults to remember back to when you were a freshman or sophomore in high school and answer the questions I will ask from that perspective.

Will the oldest person in the group please pick up the Fran/Fred card. I'm going to ask a question and give you time to discuss the answer briefly. The person with the card will start the discussion. When I call time, the card will be passed one person to the left, and the new card-holder will begin the discussion on the second question. Remember, Fran/Fred is a person of the opposite gender who is just a friend; Ida/Ike is a person for whom you have special sexual infatuation.

2. *Give one question below, allow enough time for a very short discussion, then say "Pass the card" and give the next question. Keep the exercise moving.*

- How does it feel to talk to Fran/Fred as compared to talking to Ida/Ike?

- Would people tease you about your relationship with Fran/Fred? With Ida/Ike?

- What kind of notes would you write to Fran/Fred? to Ida/Ike?

- How would you feel if you saw Fran/Fred talking to another girl/guy? Compared to how you would feel about Ida/Ike?

- What would you tell your parents about Fran/Fred? About Ida/Ike?

- What signs of affection would you use to show Fran/Fred that you liked her/him? Signs of affection for Ida/Ike?

- How long would your relationship with Fran/Fred probably last? Your relationship with Ida/Ike?

- How would you feel if someone told you Fran/Fred said something mean about you? How about if Ida/Ike said mean things?

- How would you treat Fran/Fred when you were with your same-sex friends? How would you treat Ida/Ike?

- How comfortable would you be about telling Fran/Fred that he/she had bad breath? Ida/Ike?

- What would you do if Fran/Fred was getting into serious bad habits like alcohol or drugs? How about Ida/Ike?

- Would you go to church with Fran/Fred? With Ida/Ike?

3. *When you have completed the questions above, say:*

> Based on your responses, discuss the difference between Friendship and Infatuation in the lives of adolescents.

C. Touch: Love or Exploitation

Invite the young people to bring their chairs and move up close to you and to the board. Then invite the adults to bring their chairs and move in behind the teens. Distribute the *Parent Handout* (pages 150–151) outlining for the parents the material you will be presenting in this part of the session.

1. *Write on the board: **N >> T >> HH >> H+K >> PK >> ST >> SI.** See if anyone can tell you what this set of letters might mean, then say:*

> An infatuation relationship usually follows a certain pattern of development. (Point to the letters on the board as you explain them.) It moves from **noticing** a person who attracts you, to **talking** to the person, to **holding hands**, to **hugging and kissing**, to **passionate kissing**, to **sexual touching**, to **sexual intercourse**.

2. *Continue dialoguing with the group using the following questions:*

> *How long does it take to move from the beginning of this line to the end?*

(Field a few answers from the group. Point out that in many movies and shows, the line goes from N to SI in a few hours.)

> *What moves the line forward?*

(Explain that this line moves forward in response to hormones: testosterone in the male, estrogen and progesterone in the female. The hormones trigger powerful responses in the body that drive the body forward along the line.)

What controls the power of the sex drive? If our hormones are so powerful, why don't we have sex with every person we are attracted to?

(Field a few answers to this question, then say: The best answer to that question is in the next line.)

3. *Under the line above write the following: S >> A >> C >> F >> IF >> RL. Space the letters so the RL ends up under the ST and SI. See if anyone can tell you what the letters mean, then say:*

> This is the pattern that shows the growth of a relationship from Friendship to Love. This line moves from being **strangers,** to **acquaintances,** to **classmates, companions, chums** (people we hang around with at school), to **friends** (we know their families, we go to their homes), to **intimate friends** (people we tell our deepest secrets to), to **real love.**

4. *Ask the group the following:*

> How long does it take to move from the beginning of this line to the end? What moves this line forward? (Help the group to see that this line's progress depends on spending time together, mutual interests, honest communication, caring, commitment, and forgiveness. It takes a long time, maybe years, for a relationship to grow from S to RL.)

5. *Explain more about romantic relationships using the following words:*

> Most romantic relationships are a combination of these two lines, the **Infatuation** and the **Friendship/Love** lines. We can call it **The Big IF.** If the Friendship-to-Love line (point to the line on the board) is in control, the relationship is probably healthy; if the Infatuation factor (point to the I line) is in control, the relationship will very readily get into sexual trouble.

> Each step on the **I** line is meant by God to be the expression of a deepening *love* relationship, with the signs of love becoming more and more intimate as the relationship deepens. When the steps on the line are really signs of Love, it is love that controls the hormones. Real Love puts a spiritual heart around the last two steps and saves them for marriage. (Draw a heart that takes in the SI and ST and the RL below them and write **MARRIAGE** above the heart.)

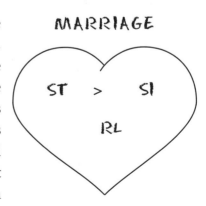

6. *Summarize the material presented to this point. Say:*

Movement along the Infatuation line can have two very different meanings—love and lust.

As *love*, the steps along the I-line are meant to be the external signs of a deepening love relationship.

As *lust*, the movement along the line can be simply a physical response to hormones, without any real regard for the other person or for one's own best interests and values. When the steps on the line are acts of lust, the person thinks only about himself or herself, and *uses* the other person for his/her own purposes—such as pleasure or power or anger. Other words for this kind of activity are **sexual exploitation** or **sexual abuse**.

In an actual relationship, however, it is sometimes very difficult to tell the difference between love and lust. Sometimes the movement along the I-line begins as a true expression of affection and becomes exploitation somewhere along the line.

7. *Explain three categories of sexual exploitation. Say:*

So when does infatuation become exploitation? There is an important distinction to make here between what I would call three categories of sexual exploitation.

8. *Write a big **E** on the board and say:*

Some sexual activity is just plain exploitation. Pedophilia always fits in this category. Rape does, too. And some of the sexual things teens do fit here as well. Four examples include: A recent news report about a group of senior boys who were putting notches in their belts every time they "scored" with a freshman girl; a group of cheerleaders bragging about how much fun they would have "playing with" the freshman basketball players to see how far they could get them to go; a sophomore boy explaining to his friends: "All you have to do is take a girl's hand, look into her eyes, and say 'I love you,' and she will do anything you want her to do"; a recent TV report that teen girls had decided that they could be "players" just as much as the boys could.

9. *Write a big **IF** on the board and say:*

> Many times sexual abuse fits into this second category—what starts out as an honest display of affection *becomes* exploitation. In this instance, the dating couple does not intend to use each other. They are honestly intending to show their growing affection for one another. But "one thing leads to another," their hormones take over, and they get involved with signs of affection that are farther along the line than their love relationship. Date rape can fit here. But so can any experience of "going too far."

10. *Write a big **F** on the board and say:*

> There is a new phenomenon in the teen world today that is another form of sexual exploitation—something your peers might call "friends with benefits." What it means is that some girls (or guys) are willing to do sexual things—often oral sex—as a "favor" for a person who is a friend or even just an acquaintance. This is simply another new kind of exploitation and is not really a "benefit" to anyone. Experimenting with sex with a friend or group of friends also fits into this category.

> We can sum up this whole discussion about love and lust in two rules (transparencies 155–156):

> **If it isn't real love—DON'T.**

> **If it is real love—WAIT.**

11. *Give everyone, teens and parents, a copy of the handout* Teen World Realities, *a lap board, and a pen. Say to the teens:*

> The world you are growing up in is giving you a very different message about sex than the one we are presenting tonight. Our message is that sexual activity is meant to be saved for marriage. That is the clear teaching of the commandments and of the Church. On the other hand, the message you hear in song, TV, movies, and society is "Sex is fun. Do it now."

> This exercise is meant to help you think about which of those messages is making the biggest impact on you and your friends. At the top of this page are some of the realities that might influence you to listen to the message of the world rather than God's message. Mark these to show how much influence you think each has on the

personal values and decisions of the kids you know. Parents, mark them the way you think your child will answer. (Read the list aloud, commenting and explaining each item briefly. Tell the group not to do the bottom of the page until you explain it.)

12. *Say to the parents:*

> The top list shows the reality of the teen world. I am sure that you as parents want to protect your child from all of this. Every one of you wants your sons and daughters to get through their teen years without being hurt sexually—or without hurting someone else. You want your child to develop a deep love relationship that will someday be celebrated in a beautiful marriage and will produce a loving family. What can you do to help make all of this happen?

> At the bottom of the page is a list of the things that teens need in their lives if they are going to be able to control the negative realities above and develop good, healthy romantic relationships. Parents, mark the items below to show how strong an influence you feel each is having on your child's decision making. Teens, mark them to show what influence you think each item actually has in your life at this time.

Allow time, then invite the parents and teens to get together to compare their answers and discuss any differences.

D. Feedback and LIFE Report Card

Give everyone a Feedback Sheet, pen, lap board, and a copy of the *LIFE Report Card* (page 152–153).

1. *Say:*

> When I have finished giving directions, you will complete the Feedback Sheet first. What you write will be completely confidential. You may sign your name or leave it anonymous. I will collect the Feedback Sheets later.

> After you finish the Feedback Sheet, I invite you to fill out the *LIFE Report Card*. Look at the report card now. It gives you a chance to think about how well you are doing at the life-long task of learning to love. Notice in the grading system that the A's, B's, and C's have a special meaning. We will not be asking you to share what you write on the report card at this time, but you may want to share it with your family members when you get home.

Notice that there are four grading periods. You will be marking the first column now. I encourage you to take the report card out again at two-week intervals and see if you have shown any improvement in any of the areas.

Parents, you will notice that the report card is written to fit the lives of teenagers. As you read through the items, you can mentally make the adjustments needed to fit your own stage of growth.

Invite everyone to find a quiet spot in the room where they can write privately. Allow time for writing.

2. *Allow five to ten minutes for follow up.*

Collect the Feedback Sheets. Read some of the responses orally, answering questions as there is time. (Be careful not to read aloud anything that would be of a confidential nature.)

Respond at a later time to any serious problems that might have surfaced on the Feedback Sheets (see page 154).

E. Closing Prayer

Gather in the large-group setting. Distribute copies of the 1 Corinthians 13 Prayer (page 149).

1. *Say:*

God made us for love. Learning to love is the most important thing any of us can do in our lives. One of the most profound teachings about love ever written can be found in a letter written by Paul many, many years ago to a group of Christians in the city of Corinth.

2. *Read the passage aloud, then say:*

Now, please read the passage through again silently as a kind of examination of conscience. For each phrase ask yourself—Am I patient? Am I kind? Am I jealous? etc. Then thank God for all the ways you have already learned to show love in your family and friendship relationships and ask God to help you to be a more loving person.

Allow time for silent reflection. Then invite everyone to read the passage aloud as your closing.

Fran / Fred
(FRIENDSHIP)

Ike / Ida
(INFATUATION)

Fran / Fred
(FRIENDSHIP)

Ike / Ida
(INFATUATION)

Fran / Fred
(FRIENDSHIP)

Ike / Ida
(INFATUATION)

Fran / Fred
(FRIENDSHIP)

Ike / Ida
(INFATUATION)

TEEN WORLD REALITIES

Listed below are some of the realities in today's world that push teens to "go too far" along the line of sexual activity. Indicate how much influence each of the items has on the decisions of your peers..

V = Very strong influence
S = Some influence
N = No influence (or little)

____ Curiosity about sexual things
____ Hormones
____ Peer pressure
____ Fun, parties
____ Alcohol, drugs
____ Independence, cars
____ Sense of power: wanting to be studs, players
____ Expectations of society: media, books
____ Easy access to condoms, birth control

Listed below are some of the realities teens need to control the factors above and to develop healthy romantic relationships. Indicate how much influence each of these factors has on your personal decisions regarding dating and sexuality. Use the same code as above.

____ Good communication with parents about sexual things
____ Clear expectations and rules for parties and dating
____ Family support: honest, loving relationships with parents, siblings, extended family
____ Peer support: strong friendships with members of both genders; good example from friends
____ Wholesome fun, parties, dances
____ Faith, prayer, Church teachings
____ Accurate information about male and female anatomy, hormones, contraception, STDs
____ Monitored exposure to movies, TV, videos, books, magazines
____ Personal morals, strong commitments, clear goals
____ Reverence for the sacrament of matrimony and the sacredness of sex
____ Respect for myself and my reputation
____ Respect for the other person and his/her reputation
____ Awareness of the possibility of pregnancy
____ Fear of exposure to a sexually transmitted disease

Love is always patient and kind;

Love is never jealous;

Love is not boastful or conceited,

It is not rude and never seeks its own advantage;

It does not take offense or store up grievances.

Love does not rejoice at wrongdoing,

but finds its joy in truth.

It is always ready to make allowances,

to trust,

to hope,

and to endure whatever comes.

As it is, these remain:

Faith, Hope, and Love,

the three of them;

and the greatest of them is

LOVE.

1 Corinthians 13:4–7, 13 (NJB)

Learning about LIFE:
A Family-Based Program on Relationships and Abuse Prevention

For adolescents in grades 9 and 10 with their parents

Goals:

- To help adolescents understand four basic kinds of relationships—Love, Infatuation, Friendship, and Exploitation—and the difference between them.

- To help adolescents understand that one of the major aspects of becoming an adult is learning how to give and receive love.

- To help adolescents understand, and deal appropriately with, sexual attraction and relationships that have a sexual component.

- To help adolescents understand the feelings associated with the various kinds of relationship and the kinds of touch used to express each.

- To help adolescents become aware of the reality of sexual abuse as a major form of exploitation

- To help adolescents realize that some sexually-related activities that they or their peers are involved in can be exploitative and abusive.

- To teach adolescents how to respond to any experience of sexual abuse—past, present, or future.

- To begin the healing process for any adolescent who may have been abused in the past.

Four basic kinds of human relationship: LIFE

Love: Love is the most beautiful, the most rewarding, and the most challenging of all relationships. Love involves mutual acceptance, respect, and trust. Love shows itself in commitment and a willingness to sacrifice for the one loved. Love is enduring, patient, forgiving, and encouraging. Love lasts through thick and thin. Learning to give and to receive love is the most important task any human being faces.

Infatuation (or being "in love"): Romantic infatuation is a relationship involving deep emotion and sexual attraction. Infatuation is exciting and all-absorbing. It is characterized by extremes of happiness and dejection, by exclusiveness and jealousy. Infatuation seeks expression in kisses, hugs, touches, and sometimes sexual intercourse. Infatuation is often called "love," but it isn't the same as love. Unless it is accompanied by real love, infatuation won't last.

How would a person feel who has been sexually abused?

The response of children and adolescents to sexual abuse is often CONFUSION. They may have many negative feelings like shame, embarrassment, guilt, hurt, and betrayal. But they may also have some good feelings. Sexual touch is supposed to be a pleasant experience. The abuser may be gentle and seem to be loving. The victims might believe what the abuser has said to them, and feel special and loved. Sometimes the victims don't realize until much later that they have been lied to and used.

What does a person who has been (or is being) sexually abused need to know?

Sexual abuse can cause serious traumatic problems in the life of a person who has been abused. Anyone who has been—or is being—abused needs to remember these things:

- God loves you very much, and wants you to be healed of the bad effects of this traumatic experience in your life.

- You are a good and lovable person. The person who abused you did a bad thing to you, but that did not make you a bad person.

- It is important that you tell an adult whom you trust. Those who love you can't help you unless they know what happened. If you tell someone and that person doesn't believe you, keep telling until you find someone who will listen.

- The sexual abuse is not your fault. An abuser will try to blame you for what happened, but the abuse is the adult's fault, not yours.

- Sexual abuse is like a serious wound that needs to be healed. The healing might take a long time and much counseling and guidance. Those who love you can help you to get better, but you must let them help.

- If a friend tells you that they are being abused, you *must* find an adult who can help the friend. This is a problem that is much too big for an adolescent to try to solve.

God is love,
and all who live in love
live in God
and God in them.

There is an important distinction to make here between three categories of sexual exploitation.

1. Some sexual activity is just plain exploitation. One person deliberately *uses* another for his or her own purposes. Pedophilia always fits in this category. Rape does as well. And so some of the sexual things teens do to and with one another.

2. Many times sexual abuse fits into this second category—what starts out as an honest display of affection *becomes* exploitation. In this instance, the dating couple do not intend to use each other. They are honestly intending to show their growing affection for one another. But "one thing leads to another," their hormones take over, and they get involved with signs of affection that are farther along the line than their love relationship. Date rape can fit in here. But so can many experiences of "going too far."

3. There is a new phenomenon in the teen world today that is another form of sexual exploitation—something called "friends with benefits." Some girls (or guys) are willing to do sexual things—often oral sex—as a "favor" for a person who is a friend or even just an acquaintance. This is simply another kind of exploitation and is not a "benefit" to anyone. Experimentation with sex with a friend or group of friends also fits into this category. The whole discussion about sexual activity can be summed up in two rules:

If it isn't real love—DON'T.
If it is real love—WAIT.

Friendship: Friendship is comfortable and easy, enriching and fun. It is based on mutual trust, understanding, acceptance, and enjoyment. Friendship is not exclusive or possessive but leaves the other free. A person can have many friends at once, friends of both sexes, friends of all ages, races, and religions. Some friendships last a lifetime. The best of them grow into love.

Exploitation: Exploitation is a relationship based on selfishness. We exploit others when we use them to get what we want and don't really care how they think or feel. Exploitative relationships lack respect, concern, and commitment; they are deceptive and self-serving. Manipulation, ridicule, abuse, blackmail, pranks, vandalism, and casual sex are all forms of exploitation. If we are honest, we can discover some degree of exploitation in most of our relationships.

Touch—Love or Exploitation

N >> T >> HH >> H+K >> PK >> ST >> SI

An Infatuation relationship usually follows a certain pattern of development. It moves from **noticing** a person who attracts you, to **talking** to the person, to **holding hands,** to **hugging and kissing,** to **passionate kissing,** to **sexual touching,** to **sexual intercourse.**

S >> A >> C >> F >> IF >> RL

The second pattern shows the growth of a relationship from Friendship to Love. It moves from being **strangers,** to **acquaintances,** to **classmates, companions, chums** (people we hang around with at school), to **friends** (we know their families, we go to their homes), to **intimate friends** (people we tell our deepest secrets to), to **real love** (we are willing to sacrifice even our lives for their good).

The Infatuation line can have two very different meanings—love and lust.

• As **love,** the steps along the I-line are meant by God to be the external signs of a deepening love relationship.

• As **lust,** the movement along the line can be simply a physical response to hormones, without any real regard for the other person or for one's own best interests and values. When the steps on the line are acts of lust, the person thinks only about himself or herself, and *uses* the other person for his or her own purposes—such as pleasure or power or anger. Another word for this kind of activity is **sexual exploitation** or **sexual abuse.**

EXPLOITATION

If we look closely at any of our relationships, we can probably find some degree of exploitation there. Exploitation is using others for our own selfish purposes. We use people who are our friends and people we don't like so well. Sometimes we exploit people deliberately; sometimes we aren't even aware that our conduct is exploitative. Some forms of exploitation are minor, some are major, and some are even criminal.

Listed below are kinds of exploitation that might be found in the life of an adolescent your age. DO NOT WRITE your responses. Just read through the list as a kind of examination of conscience. Then pray about any negative aspects of your character that the list reveals to you. Ask God to forgive you, to help you to overcome your selfishness, and to guide your efforts to become a more loving person.

- making fun of people
- blaming others for things that are your own fault
- teasing others in a negative way
- borrowing things and not paying them back
- tattling on someone just to get them in trouble
- gossiping about someone—especially on the Internet
- laughing at someone's mistake or accident
- making prank phone calls
- betraying the trust someone has in you
- telling a secret you promised to keep
- winning a game by cheating or breaking the rules
- using one parent against the other
- being nice to someone just to get what you want from them
- reading someone's private letters or diary
- telling lies about someone
- stealing and vandalism
- hot dogging, hogging the ball
- blackmailing someone
- bullying
- ganging up on someone
- encouraging someone to use alcohol or other drugs
- experimenting sexually
- leading a person on to see how far he or she will go
- threatening bodily harm if someone tells on you
- taking advantage of someone

Your LIFE Report Card

The items below will help you to grade your growth as a loving person. Use the first column to grade yourself now. Then decide on one or two areas that you want to improve in and promise yourself that you will work on these. Set another "grading period," at least two weeks away, when you will measure the success of your efforts by grading yourself again. There is space for you to do that three more times.

Use the following grading code:

A = Almost Always; Amazingly good progress

B = Best effort; Better than before

C = Could Care more

D = Doesn't really try

F = Frequently Forgets

LOVE

God created us human beings for love. We spend our entire lifetime learning how to love God, love one another, and love ourselves. We gradually learn, both how to give love and how to receive it. Most of what we learn about loving and being loved, we learn in the school called "family." Grade yourself as a loving member of your family.

I show my affection for my family members with hugs, kisses, and loving words.

I appreciate my family and often thank them for the things they do for me.

I try to understand how the other people in my family feel and think of ways to make them happy.

I am willing to admit my mistakes, to ask forgiveness, and to forgive my family when they annoy or hurt me.

I am truthful and honest with my family; I tell my parents what I am doing and where I am going.

I willingly spend time with my family: talking, playing games, and having fun together.

I listen to the guidance given to me by my parents and accept their corrections respectfully.

I do my share of the family chores responsibly, willingly, and cheerfully.

I respect the privacy and belongings of the other members of my family.

I pray for my family every day and pray with them at home and in church.

INFATUATION: "The I-Factor"

One of the primary growing tasks of the teen years is learning how to deal with infatuation. (We are using that term here to stand for sexual attraction in any degree—from just being "interested" in a person of the other gender, all the way to being sexually "intimate" with someone.) As our bodies mature, they begin to produce hormones that cause the physical changes associated with sexuality. These hormones also create sexual feelings, interests, and desires. Each individual has to learn how to understand these sexual urges and how to respond to them appropriately in ways that are loving and life-giving.

Grade yourself on how well you have learned the "I-Tasks" listed below.

I am comfortable carrying on a conversation and doing school activities with members of the other gender.			
When I have questions about sexual matters, I ask my parents or some other trusted adult.			
I stay away from movies, TV, videos, and websites that exploit sexuality as something dirty and bad.			
During a prayer or game, I can take the hand of a person of the other gender without getting nervous or silly.			
I stay away from parties that might involve alcohol, drugs, or any kind of exploitative sexual activity.			
I am able to talk to a person of the other gender about my feelings and inner thoughts.			
I try to understand how members of the other gender think and feel about various things.			
I refrain from teasing my peers when they have a boyfriend or girlfriend.			
I understand why parties or other activities involving both genders need to be chaperoned.			
I make my choices regarding my sexuality based on what I know is right and not on the expectations of my friends.			
I ask God to help me to make positive, life-giving choices in my relationships with members of the other gender.			
I respect the moral choices of my boyfriend or girlfriend.			
I refrain from being a source of sexual temptation by how I dress and act.			

FRIENDSHIP

You have been learning about the relationship called friendship since you were a very young child. You have learned by experience such things as: how to make friends, how to be a friend, how to deal with a friend who is having problems, what to do when a friend wants you to do things you don't want to do, how to make up with a friend after a quarrel or fight.
The list below tells some of the things a good friend does. Use the list to grade yourself as a friend.

Good friends

Think of fun and interesting things to do with their friends.			
Spend time with their friends doing the things their friends want to do.			
Would tell their parents if their friends were doing something seriously wrong.			
Influence their friends to do the right thing.			
Encourage their friends not to do things that would get them in trouble.			
Cheer their friends up when they are hurt, sad, or unhappy.			
Help their friends to be polite and respectful to adults.			
Help their friends be friendly and kind to other kids.			
Encourage their friends to follow classroom and school rules.			
Encourage and help their friends to do their best in class work and homework.			
Are happy with their friends when they do well in activities: sports, music, plays, etc.			
Apologize when they have been hurtful, mean, or angry with their friends.			
Forgive their friends when they apologize for being hurtful or angry.			
Can be trusted to keep secrets shared with them.			
Tell their friends off (respectfully) when they deserve it.			
Are loyal—don't talk about their friends behind their backs.			
Listen when their friends have something important to talk about.			
Pray for and with their friends.			

FEEDBACK SHEET

Please circle one: father, mother, boy, girl

1. How did you feel about this lesson? What did you learn that you didn't know before?

2. Will this lesson help you to make decisions for your own life as a parent or as a child? Explain your answer.

3. If you have a question you want me to answer to the whole group, write it here:

4. If you would like to talk to someone about anything you heard tonight, please write your name and phone number below.

Or tear here and call one of these numbers:

IF IT ISN'T

REAL LOVE—

DON'T

IF IT IS

REAL LOVE—

WAIT

Other Titles of Interest

Sex and the Teenager
Choices and Decisions
Kieran Sawyer, S.S.N.D.
Through the presentation of a Catholic Christian perspective, *Sex and the Teenager* has a clear, straightforward goal: to encourage teens to say "no" to premarital sexual intercourse and to avoid such serious problems as teen pregnancy and sexually trasmitted diseases.
PARTICIPANT BOOK:
ISBN: 0-87793-681-1 / 112 pages / $7.95 / Ave Maria Press
LEADER'S MANUAL:
ISBN: 0-87793-682-X / 168 pages, 8 ½" x 11", spiral bound / $21.95 / Ave Maria Press

Sex, Love, and You
Making the Right Decision
Tom and Judy Lickona, with William Boudreau, M.D.
Rooted in the Judeo-Christian tradition, this book promotes the value of chastity to teens. In a direct, no-nonsense fashion, the authors examine the dangers of sexual activity and the rewards of abstinence.
ISBN: 0-87793-987-X / 192 pages, photos / $11.95 / Ave Maria Press

10 Best Gifts for Your Teen
Raising Teens with Love and Understanding
Patt and Steve Saso
The Sasos combine their expertise as a counselor and high school teacher with wisdom from their own experience as parents to offer practical and effective guidance for the parents of teens. Included in this book are the encouragement and skills parents need to build strong relationships with their teens.
ISBN: 1-893732-05-3 / 144 pages / $12.95 / Sorin Books

Coaching Character at Home
Strategies for Raising Responsible Teens
Michael Koehler, Ph.D.
Successful coaches know that character is the core of every winner, and consistency is the key to character. Koehler reinforces the parental roles and shares the Seven C's of character: Connectedness, Control, Commitment, Consistencey, Cooperation, Conscience, Competition.
ISBN: 1-893732-48-7 / 224 pages / $14.95 / Sorin Books

Raising Courageous Kids
Eight Steps to Practical Heroism
Charles A. Smith, Ph.D.
Dr. Smith explains how courage develops in eight stages from birth to early adolescence. He also provides solid information and practical ideas to help nurture courage at every one of these stages.
ISBN: 1-893732-76-2 / 224 pages / $14.95 / Sorin Books

Available from your local bookstore or from **ave maria press**
Notre Dame, IN 46556 / www.avemariapress.com
ph: 1.800.282.1865 / fax: 1.800.282.5681
Prices and availability subject to change.

Keycode: FØTØ5Ø6ØØØØ